A Collector's Guide To
Paper Dolls
Saalfield, Lowe, Merrill

By

Mary Young

_To Michaele Mueller -
With My Best Wishes
Mary Young_

COLLECTOR BOOKS
P.O. Box 3009
Paducah, Kentucky 42001

Dedication

To my husband George and our five children, Carol, Wendy, Lorrie, Linda, and George Jr. (Skip).
To Mrs. Samuel Lowe and her family.
To Mr. Henry Saalfield and his family.
To Miss Alice McQuistion.

Acknowledgements

I would like to thank the following for their help in sending me information for use in this book, and loaning me their paper dolls for picturing. Virginia Crossley, Emma Terry, Audrey Sepponen, Betsy Slap, Bob Kelly, Jean Woodcock, Shirley Hedge, Pearl Silzly, Bonnie Fuson, Marge Meisinger, Norene McDonald, Mary Kelley, Edith Lowe, Dean Keller, Henry Saalfield, Louise Rumely, Marilyn Johnson, Pam Hunter, Ruth Garfinkel, Estelle Spyes, Betsy Addison, Richard Rusnock, Dot Trippel, Edith Linn, Grayce Piemontesi, Bette Wells, Jane Sugg, Gladys McGill, Jean Vandiver, Shirley Edgerly, Jeannine Gliwski, Kassey Ferguson, Pat Rouillard, Eleanor Van Dyke Pearson, Elsie Stevens, and Katherine McIntire.

All Photographs By The Author Unless Noted

All Paper Dolls Pictured Are From The Authors Collection Unless Noted

Other Books By The Author

Paper Dolls and Their Artists - Book I
Paper Dolls and Their Artists - Book II

The current values in this book should be used only as a guide. They are not intended to set prices, which vary from one section of the country to another. Auction prices as well as dealer prices vary greatly and are affected by condition as well as demand. Neither the Author nor the Publisher assumes responsibility for any losses that might be incurred as a result of consulting this guide.

Printed by IMAGE GRAPHICS, Paducah, Kentucky

Introduction

The main purpose of this book is to identify all the paper dolls published in the United States commercially since 1900. Because of the great quantity of paper dolls produced in this country it is impossible to publish everything in one volume. This book covers the paper dolls published by three of the major companies; Saalfield, Lowe and Merrill. All known original paper dolls and their reprints are listed and all of the listed originals are pictured.

Because many paper doll collectors also collect books and box sets of paper toys and stand-ups of dolls, animals, toys, etc., these are also included in the general lists when they are known. It should be understood, though, that they do not contain paper dolls with outfits, and they will not be pictured in the picture sections.

The books in the picture sections and general lists are listed in numerical order according to the publishers number which appears on the book cover. If the book has no number, then the book is listed at the end of the list. Most numbers are 3 or 4 digit numbers. Occasionally you may find a number on a book reading as follows: 2723:15. The 15 is not part of the number but merely the publisher's code for the price of the book; i.e., 15ᶜ.

The general lists will serve as a check list for all the original and reprint books. Concerning the reprints, the list also includes, in most cases the number of the original book from which it came.

Price Guide

The prices in this book are based on mint, uncut, original paper dolls. Reprints that are almost identical are just slightly lower in price. In the case of a reprint of a celebrity book where the dolls have been redrawn, the price is drastically reduced. There are a few rare cases of a reprint having a higher value than its original. Such is the case of a few non-celebrity books by the Lowe Company that were reprinted with redrawn dolls and made into celebrity books.

Cut sets are usually half the price of the uncut set providing that all the dolls and outfits are included and the pieces are in very good condition. If, however, any dolls or outfits are missing, bent, mended, or torn, etc., the price decreases accordingly.

The prices in this guide were largely derived from many detailed studies of different sales lists of paper dolls and notes taken at paper doll conventions where paper dolls were sold. Information and knowledge from other collectors and personal judgement were other influencing factors.

Paper Doll Collecting

Readers unfamiliar with the recent hobby of paper doll collecting may wonder at the interest of avid paper doll collectors. Although paper doll collecting may not seem an inspiring pastime to some, collectors have found the historical and cultural value of the paper doll to be not only fascinating, but enjoyable as well.

Adults who remember the happy hours of enjoyment paper dolls brought them as a child need only to meet or hear of another paper doll collector to get caught up in this hobby. Even those who never played with paper dolls become infatuated with the hobby, some just because they are interested in the dress designs of past eras.

Paper doll collecting has been growing rapidly in recent years, getting a good start in the 1960's. Collectors range in age from small children to those in their 80's and 90's. Not everyone collects the same type of paper dolls. As with other hobbies, everyone has different interests. Some collect only the celebrity paper dolls, while others like only the non-celebrity. Some like only the un-cut paper dolls, while others like them cut out. There are some collectors who collect only the paper dolls that appeared in magazines or newspapers and then there are others who, like myself, collect just about all the different kinds of paper dolls there are!

No one knows for sure just how paper dolls were originated. One popular belief is that they began as pantins (jumping jacks) in Europe. Pantins were dolls made of cardboard with arms and legs that moved when a string attached to the parts was pulled.

Paper dolls during the 19th century were of famous dancers and of the opera star, Jenny Lind, plus many of the non-celebrity kind, all of which are very rare and hard to find now. In the late 1800's the Raphael Tuck Publishers in England produced many beautiful series of paper dolls. These were distributed in the United States through their New York office.

Advertising paper dolls were used by many companies in the late 1800's to further the sale of their products. The ONT Thread Company, Lion Coffee, McLoughlins Coffee, Ceresota Flour, and Pillsbury Flour are a few samples. Many times the child could send away for a complete series of paper dolls after receiving the first doll with the product. This type of advertising continued into the 1900's and even today has not completely disappeared.

Around the turn of the century popular women's magazines started to include a page of paper dolls. The most popular were *Ladies' Home Journal*, *Good Housekeeping*, *Pictorial Review*, *McCall's*, *Delineator* and *Woman's Home Companion*. The *McCall's Magazine* still features paper dolls occasionally, of Betsy McCall.

From the beginning, commercial paper dolls could be bought in books, boxes, envelopes or folders; but the type of paper dolls most familiar to us today is the paper doll book which features the dolls on the cardboard covers and the clothes on the inside pages. This type of book made its appearance in the late 1920's and the early 1930's and sold for a very reasonable price of either five or ten cents. This meant that children everywhere in the country could enjoy paper dolls with their saved pennies. Even during the depression years these books sold well and parents could buy paper dolls for birthdays and holidays for a fraction of what "real" dolls sold for.

The various companies that produced the paper dolls were very encouraged with the excellent response to the paper doll books and started publishing more and more of these books. The war years of the early 1940's saw the biggest surge of paper dolls which was never to be equaled again. Every company seemed to try to outdo one another with beautiful books of non-celebrity and celebrity paper dolls. Some celebrity books from those years are Alice Fay, Claudette Colbert, Judy Garland, Greer Garson and Rita Hayworth, not to mention the child stars of Margaret O'Brien and Gloria Jean. Shirley Temple was a teenager by now; however, many paper dolls of Shirley as a child appeared in the 1930's and one set as a teenager in the 1940's. There were paper dolls of the stars of radio programs such as "Hour of Charm", "Glenn Miller" and "Benny Goodman" plus paper dolls from entire movies such as "Ziegfeld Girl" and "Gone With The Wind". One book called *Hollywood Personalities* featured the stars from the Bing Crosby movie "Holiday Inn".

Aside from the paper doll books, children of the 1930's and 1940's also enjoyed paper dolls that appeared in the comic sections of their local newspapers. "Blondie", "Brenda Star" and "Jane Arden" were very popular at that time, and children eagerly awaited the Sunday comics to get their new paper dolls.

Paper dolls were still produced in good quantities in the 1950's. However, the advent of television was being felt and children were not quite as interested in sitting down to read a good book or cut out paper dolls as before. From the 1960's on, there has been a steady decline in the amount of paper dolls produced. However, you will find some in your local stores in lesser quantity. The more recent paper dolls in the celebrity category are those from the television shows of "The Brady Bunch", "The Partridge Family" and "The Waltons". Paper dolls of "real" dolls were made as far back as the 1930's. The Dy-Dee-Doll is one example. Recently there have been dozens of this type of paper doll, with the Barbie Doll well out in front.

It is often asked how one goes about starting a paper doll collection. If you are interested in starting a general collection, begin by buying the paper dolls available in the stores now. Someday these will be sought after also. If you want to concentrate on paper dolls from a special era or one particular type of paper doll, make a point to visit flea markets, antique shows and even garage sales. You may also want to check with friends and neighbors. They might have a box of paper dolls from their childhood stored away in the attic just waiting for you!

On The Subject Of Reprints

Very often an original paper doll book was reprinted after it was published. Sometimes the book was reprinted exactly like the original, but more often it was changed somewhat. The following typifies the many different ways an original may have been reprinted:

The reprint and original may be exact duplicates.
The reprint may be an exact duplicate but with a different price.
The reprint may be the same but with no price on the book at all.
The reprint may have fewer pages.
The reprint may be printed on a lesser grade of paper.
The reprint may have a new background on the covers; dolls and inside pages remain the same.
The reprint may have completely new covers, dolls redrawn while inside pages remain the same.
The reprint may have fewer dolls than the original.
The reprint may have the original dolls plus some added new dolls.
The reprint may have a different title than the original.
The reprint may be a box set while the original was a book.
The reprint may be a book while the original was a box set.
The reprint may be made up of dolls from two, three or even four different paper doll books.
The reprint may have dolls and outfits of reduced or enlarged size.
The reprint may not have die-cut dolls though the original book did.
The reprint may have coloring pages added or subtracted.
The reprint may have a reprint of its own.
The reprint may be an exact duplicate but with a different trade name.

One common type of reprint is better known in the business as a jobber book and was used by the Saalfield and Lowe companies. The Lowe Company used the trade name of "Abbott" for their jobber books. The dolls and clothes in these books were the same as the original except that usually two or more pages were dropped and the covers were made of very lightweight cardboard very seldom die-cut. The jobber book was usually placed on the market at the same time as the original main line book; however, these less expensive books did not go to the big chain stores but rather to small toy and variety stores, drug stores, train stations and bus depots.

An example of a reprint book having re-drawn dolls is *STAR BRIGHT* #1308 shown here with the original book of Sheree North, #4420 Saalfield 1957. Sheree North has four dolls, but you will notice in the reprint only three of the dolls are used. Also, the dolls have been redrawn, but they are in the same poses as the original dolls.

#4420   Courtesy of Emma Terry   #1308   Courtesy of Emma Terry

An interesting example of a reprint that has a reprint is that of a Saalfield book *THE WELL DRESSED GIRL* #2596. This book is a reprint of the Claudette Colbert book #2451. It was the usual reprint of a celebrity book made into a non-celebrity book in which the dolls were redrawn using the outlines of the Claudette Colbert dolls and retaining the original clothes. Later, it was decided to reprint *THE WELL DRESSED GIRL* and this time the clothes of Claudette Colbert were not used but new outfits were created. So, all that was left now of the Claudette Colbert book were the outlines of the dolls. This new reprint was again called *THE WELL DRESSED GIRL* with a new number #1721 (*THE WELL DRESSED GIRL* was also issued with the following numbers -#1574, #1771 and #2607.) The story does not end here as another reprint was made. A new set of dolls was drawn, and a new title *LUCKY PAPER DOLLS* (#2793 and #2693) was given the book. The dolls still maintain the basic outlines of the Claudette Colbert dolls, and the outfits are those from *THE WELL DRESSED GIRL* #1721.

Reprints may appeal to the collector just as much as the original book, especially if it contains added material or if the dolls are redrawn by a favorite artist. Many collectors try to collect both the original books and all their reprints. One paper doll book of Shirley Temple was reprinted twelve times! The original book is #4435 which was published in 1958. In the reprints the dolls are the same, but some have fewer pages of clothes. Many different cover designs can be found in the reprints. Two factors make these paper dolls of Shirley Temple not too hard to find; the number of reprints and the newness. They were reprinted from 1958 on into the Sixties.

The following is a list of the 12 most reprinted Saalfield books, some with as many as 16 reprints!

BALLET PAPER DOLLS #2616
PAPER DOLL BALLET #6093
KIDDIE CIRCUS #4430
INDIAN PAPER DOLLS #4406
HEIDI AND PETER #4187
WALTER LANTZ CARTOON SERIES #1344
PAPER DOLLS FROM MOTHER GOOSE #2758
PRESCHOOL PAPER DOLLS #6020
RAGGEDY ANN AND ANDY #2497
STORYLAND PAPER DOLLS #2798
SHIRLEY TEMPLE #4435
MY BONNIE LASSIE #4186

The Saalfield Publishing Company

The Saalfield Publishing Company was formed in 1900 when Mr. Arthur J. Saalfield purchased the publishing department of the Werner Company, a publishing and manufacturing enterprise in Akron, Ohio. Bibles, cookbooks, dictionaries, encyclopedias and home medical books were early best sellers for Saalfield.

In 1902, Mr. Saalfield published his first book for children. The book was titled *BILLY WHISKERS*. Written by Mrs. Frances Trego Montgomery, the book became the launching pad which propelled the Saalfield Company on its way to becoming one of the most successful publishers of children's books in America. Because of the success of the first *BILLY WHISKERS* book, Mrs. Montgomery was asked to write a series of *BILLY WHISKERS* books. Each of these books became a big hit with children everywhere. Other books for children, including the *AUTO BOYS* and *THE CAMPFIRE GIRL* series, were added to the Saalfield line. Mr. Saalfield's wife wrote stories for children, too, and these were published by the company under Mrs. Saalfield's maiden name of Adah Louise Sutton.

As the company grew, Mr. Saalfield began looking for more space. He also was keeping an eye out for equipment that could produce books made of cloth. He had learned of the "rag books" printed in England for very young children. Such books were just the thing for babies and toddlers because they were made of cloth and could not tear. When the Globe Sign Company in Akron went up for sale, this was heaven-sent as it not only had the larger space but also the type of equipment that Mr. Saalfield was looking for. When it was learned that the Globe Sign Company had produced advertising signs lithographed in color on muslin, Mr. Saalfield needed to look no further. The Globe Sign Company was purchased in 1906. The Saalfield Publishing Company was then moved from their old location in the Werner Company building to their new location in the Globe building. The early Saalfield muslin books soon appeared and were a big success. In 1908, a muslin book called *BABIES OF ALL NATIONS* was published. This was Saalfield's first "doll" book and it contained 12 dolls to cut out, sew and stuff. Muslin dolls were also printed on single sheets for many years, two of the earliest being *MUSLIN TEDDY BEAR* and *GREENAWAY MUSLIN DOLL*. These sheets of dolls continued for many years, and eventually there were as many as forty different sheets listed in the Saalfield catalogs. The last one, *PRISCILLA*, appeared in the 1937 catalog.

When chain stores began appearing across the country, Mr. Saalfield had the foresight to add less expensive children's books to his line. There were twelve books in the first series which included *JACK AND THE BEANSTALK* and *CINDERELLA*, and they were all illustrated by Mrs. Frances Brundage. These books were published in 1908, and it was not long before Mrs. Brundage was also drawing paper dolls for the company. She drew many of the early paper doll sets published by Saalfield.

One of the biggest successes for the company came about by the appearance into the movie world of a little girl named Shirley Temple. A contract was drawn up in 1933 which gave the Saalfield Publishing Company the exclusive rights to produce publications on Shirley Temple. Coloring books, paper dolls, story books, activity sets and other items were placed on the market and carried the company through the post depression period. Shirley Temple items sold into the 1940's and then were discontinued until late in the Fifties when Shirley Temple had her TV show. At that time, new paper dolls of Shirley as a child were produced including one paper doll that was 18 inches tall and a "Play Kit" that included paper dolls with outfits that laced onto the dolls.

The Saalfield Publishing Company was bought by the Rand McNally Company in 1976. This marked the end of three generations of publishing leadership from within the Saalfield family. When Arthur J. Saalfield died in 1919, his son Albert George Saalfield took over the company. Albert was president for forty years until his death in 1959 at which time Henry Robinson Saalfield, the son of Albert and the grandson of the founder, became president. Henry held the position until the company closed in 1976. The Saalfield archives were purchased by the Kent State University Libraries in Kent, Ohio. Here, all manner of story books, paper dolls, puzzles and games produced by the Saalfield Company will be preserved for all time.

Dean Keller, curator of Special Collections, Kent State University Libraries.

Henry Saalfield

Courtesy of Bob Kelly

THE SAALFIELD PICTURE SECTION INCLUDES PAPER DOLLS FROM THE ARTCRAFT DIVISION OF THE SAALFIELD PUBLISHING COMPANY.

Early Saalfield catalog Circa 1918.

Photo courtesy of Henry Robinson Saalfield.

Photo courtesy of Henry Robinson Saalfield.
Shirley Temple Black with Henry Robinson Saalfield at the time when the new paper dolls of Shirley were published in 1958.

Shirley Temple and Albert George Saalfield in 1938 when Shirley visited the Saalfield Publishing Company.

Assortment #2-BS.

Assortment #2-BS Box cover. $10.00

Pictured above is the box cover from assortment 2-BS, of the 1927-28 catalog and the doll it contained. Notice the title on the box "The Doll I Love Best". This title was not mentioned in the catalog, so other assortments may have titles also.

The name of the doll that came in the box is "Alice" and the name is printed at the base of the doll with the number 204. There is no date on the box or doll. The clothes sheets carry the numbers 204-B and 204-C. The coat and hat had been cut out, but obviously were 204-A.

The doll of "Alice" may also be found in book #1171, *MY BOOK OF PAPER DOLLS* with three other dolls.

Another 2-BS box has come to light, identical to the one pictured. However the doll inside is #203 Margaret. (See doll on cover of #1171.) It is the author's guess that all four dolls from the #1171 book were offered in assortment 2-BS, all using the same box cover. However, it could also be true that Margaret was just sold in the wrong box.

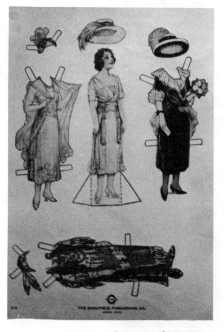

Courtesy of Jane Sugg.

Courtesy of Jane Sugg.

Pictured is a sheet from the assortment 3-A which featured the paper dolls from the book *DOLLIES TO PAINT, CUTOUT AND DRESS* #1180 which was copyrighted in 1918. These sheets measure 7¼ by 10 1/8 inches. $6.00 each sheet.

Pictured above are two sheets from the assortment 5-A. These sheets are also 7¼ by 10 1/8 inches. The sheets are of movie stars, but the stars' names do not appear on the sheets. The catalog states that there are six sheets, and the subjects consist of moving picture actors and actresses such as Charlie Chaplin and Norma Talmadge. $8.00 each sheet.

5 *BOY AND GIRL CUT-OUT DOLL BOOK*. Original copyright 1932 by the Stecher Lithographic Company. Listed in the 1937 Saalfield catalog. $25.00

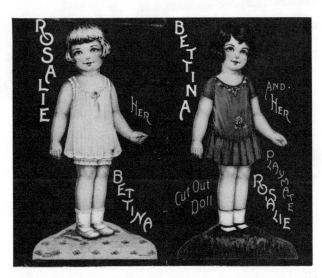

100 *BETTINA AND HER PLAYMATE ROSALIE*. Original copyright by the Stecher Lithographic Company, no date. Listed and pictured in the 1931 Saalfield catalog. $25.00

275 *BETTY JANE* 1934. $25.00.

113 *UNITED WE STAND* 1943. $15.00.

287 *DAISY'S CUT-OUT DOLL BOOK*. Listed in Saalfield catalogs of the 1920's. Book size 7½ x 10. (Book not available to picture.)

230 *PAPER DOLLS TO CUT-OUT -TEN DOLLS WITH DRESSES, HATS AND PLAYTHINGS* 1932. This book was reprinted many times with a variety of different covers and also in box sets. One reprint used this same number 230, but is dated 1939. $20.00

294 *LITTLE MARY MIXUP AND HER FRIEND PEGGY* 1922. $50.00

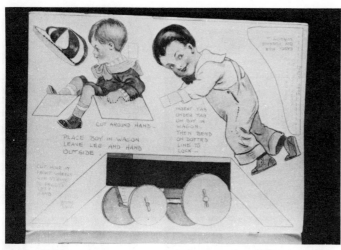

#294 - Inside page.

#294 - Inside pages.

368 *DOLLY DIMPLE.* Listed in Saalfield catalogs of the 1920's. Book size 7½ x 13½, includes doll, clothes and story. (Book not available for picture.)

368 *POLLY DOLLY.* Listed in Saalfield catalogs of the 1920's. Book size 7½ x 13½, includes doll, clothes, and story. (Book not available for picture.)

Courtesy of Betsy Slap

877 *DOLLY JEAN - HER PAPER DOLL HOUSE, FURNITURE AND CLOTHES* 1932. $25.00.

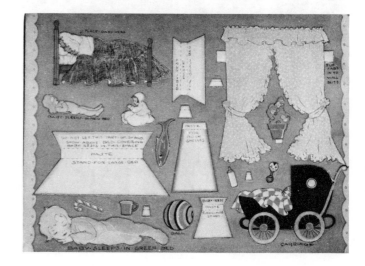

877 Back cover

#877 Inside front cover

#877 Inside back cover

881 *MANY THINGS TO DO* 1932. (One page of paper dolls.) $5.00 **Courtesy of Betsy Slap**

#956 - Inside

A PAPER DOLL WITH FIVE COSTUMES

Choose the name you like best for this little paper doll.

Mount the yellow easel on cardboard, then paste it on the doll's back so she will stand up. Cut out her pretty clothes and see how well she looks in every one of the costumes.

You will find her house and lawn furniture on other pages.

956 *SALLY LOU* 1931. $25.00

#956 - Front cover

Courtesy of Saalfield Archives.

885 *PAPER DOLLS - 180 PIECES TO CUT-OUT - TEN DOLLS WITH HATS, DRESSES AND PLAYTHINGS* 1932. $20.00

#885 Inside pages of paper dolls.

971 *LET'S PLAY STORE* 1933. (A stand-up book.) As mentioned earlier the books containing only stand-ups will not be pictured, however it was felt at least one example should be shown. This book contains 206 pieces to be put together to make a complete grocery store. There are also figures of a store keeper and three customers to stand up. The artist of this book was Fern Bisel Peat. Later in 1937 this book was reprinted with a new cover drawn by the Bailey's. The inside and back cover remained the same. This revised book is *THE GROCERY STORE* #2141. This later book was just recently reprinted by the Merrimack Publishing Corp. $20.00.

976 *DONNY DOUBLE* 1933. $20.00.

Courtesy of 1935-36 Saalfield catalog.

977 *DOTTY DOUBLE* 1933. $20.00.

980 *MICKEY MOUSE AND MINNIE MOUSE.* There are two paper doll books of Mickey and Minnie Mouse, #980 and #269. The date on #269 is verified as 1933 and is in the 1933 Saalfield catalog. In the 1934 catalog both #269 and #980 are listed. Comparing the information given in the 1934 catalog #980 is the better quality book. #980 is listed as having more pages and sold for 15¢. #269 had less pages and sold for 10¢ (in later catalogs they both sold for 10¢). Until an uncut book of #980 can be found, the date cannot be verified, although it would seem to be 1933 also. The dimensions listed in the catalogs for both books are 10 1/8 x 19½ and the pictures which appeared for both books are identical, so the dolls were the same in the two books. Price unknown.

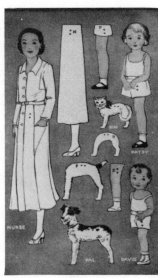

#1074 Inside front cover.

#1074 Inside back cover.

Courtesy of Emma Terry.

1074 *WALKING PAPER DOLL FAMILY* 1934. $25.00.

1171 *MY BOOK OF PAPER DOLLS -READY TO CUT-OUT AND DRESS.* This book has no date, but was listed in catalogs of the 1920's and very early 1930's. In the 1931 catalog the number was changed to #1171-804, and in the 1932 catalog the number is just #804. The last time the book is listed is in 1933. Two different covers have been found for #1171 and are pictured. View #1 has a red background and is of very stiff cardboard. View #2 is of slick paper and is signed by Frances Brundage. A linentex version of this book #936 appeared in the 1932 and 1933 editions of the Saalfield catalog and used the cover in view #1. $25.00

#1171 View #1. Courtesy of Aubrey Sepponen.

#1171 Cover view #2. Courtesy of Shirley Hedge.

#1171

#1171

Elizabeth's Trousseau

Alice's Trousseau

Mary's Trousseau

Margaret's Trousseau

Jack's Wardrobe

Helen's Trousseau

1180 *DOLLIES TO PAINT CUT-OUT AND DRESS* 1918. Included in this book are six pages of paper dolls in color and duplicate pages in black and white to be colored. $40.00.

Top left: #1180 Front cover (Back cover the same). **Courtesy of Betsy Addison. Photo by Robert Addison.**

Top center: #1180 Inside page Elizabeth's Trousseau. **Photo by Robert Addison.**

Top right: #1180 Inside page - Alice's Trousseau. **Photo by Robert Addison.**

Middle left: #1180 *INSIDE PAGE MARY'S TROUSSEAU.* **Photo by Robert Addison.**

Middle center: #1180 *INSIDE PAGE MARGARET'S TROUSSEAU.* **Photo by Robert Addison.**

Middle right: #1180 *INSIDE PAGE JACK'S WARDROBE.* **Photo by Robert Addison.**

Left: #1180 *INSIDE PAGE HELEN'S TROUSSEAU.* **Photo by Robert Addison.**

1184 *THE HAPPY FAMILY.* Listed in catalogs of the 1920's. Contains six paper dolls. Book size 8½ x 12½. (Book not available for picture.)

1261 *GULLIVER'S TRAVELS* 1939. $40.00.

Copyright Paramount Pictures, Inc. Courtesy Shirley Hedge.

1330 *MOTHER AND DAUGHTER* 1962 (date from Saalfield records). The dolls were meant to be Jackie and Caroline Kennedy. $5.00.

1331 *GINA GILLESPIE* 1962. $10.00.

#1332   Copyright Jos. L. Kallus.

#1335

#1336   Copyright Metro Goldwyn Mayer, Inc.

1332 *THE KEWPIES* 1963. $15.00.

1335 *BETTY AND HER PLAY PALS* (originated from a foreign paper doll book). $4.00.

1336 *THE WONDERFUL WORLD OF THE BROTHERS GRIMM* 1963. $10.00.

Copyright Ideal Toy Corporation. Courtesy of Virginia Crossley.
1337 *KISSY PAPER DOLL* 1963. $5.00.

Courtesy of Betsy Slap.
1339 *BONNETS AND BOWS* 1963. $4.00.

Courtesy of Louise Rumely.
1341 *BABY PAPER DOLLS* 1963. $5.00.

Courtesy of Emma Terry.
1342 *BRIDAL PARTY* 1963 $5.00.

Copyright Lantz Productions, Inc.
1344 *WALTER LANTZ CARTOON STARS* 1963 $10.00.

1345 *LITTLE WOMEN* 1963. $5.00.

1346 *PRETTY AS A ROSE* 1963. $5.00.

#1352

Copyright Kayro-Vue Productions.

1357 *CHARMING PUNCH-OUT PAPER DOLLS.* (Originated from a foreign book.) $3.00.

1352 *THE QUINTUPLETS* 1964. $6.00.

1357 *KAREN* 1965. From the Karen segment of the Television Series "90 Bristol Court" filmed at Universal Studios. $10.00.

Courtesy of Virginia Crossley.

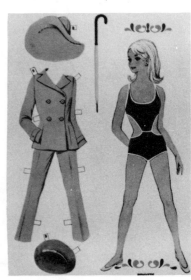

#1357. Inside cover.

1661 *GLORIA JEAN* 1940. $30.00

Copyright Universal Pictures, Inc. Courtesy of Emma Terry.

1664 *GLORIA JEAN* 1941. $40.00

Copyright Universal Pictures, Inc.

1666 *GLORIA JEAN* 1941. $40.00

Copyright Universal Pictures, Inc. Courtesy of Audrey Sepponen.

#1710

#1711

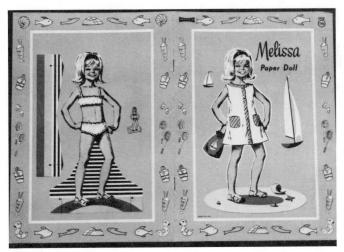

#1712

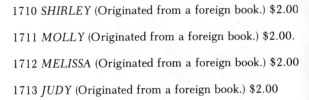

1710 *SHIRLEY* (Originated from a foreign book.) $2.00

1711 *MOLLY* (Originated from a foreign book.) $2.00.

1712 *MELISSA* (Originated from a foreign book.) $2.00

1713 *JUDY* (Originated from a foreign book.) $2.00

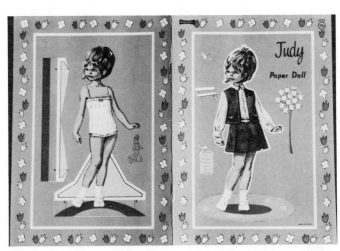

#1713   **Courtesy of Marilyn Johnson.**

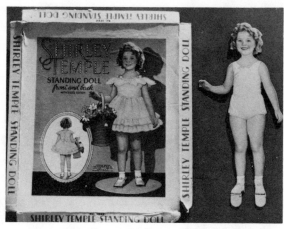

Courtesy of Audrey Sepponen.

Courtesy of Marge Meisinger.

1715 *SHIRLEY TEMPLE STANDING DOLLS* 1935 $50.00 & up.

1727 *SHIRLEY TEMPLE STANDING DOLL.* Front and back doll and clothes. 1935 - Box. $35.00

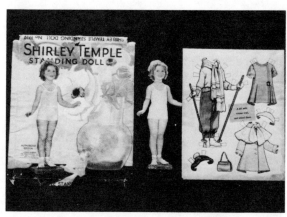

#1715 Reverse side of front cover and first page of clothes.

1719 *SHIRLEY TEMPLE STANDING DOLL* 1935 - BOX. $35.00

1728 *SHIRLEY TEMPLE DOLLS.* Listed in 1939 catalog which states the box contains two 14½" dolls. This set is not available for picturing, but most likely is a reprint of another set.

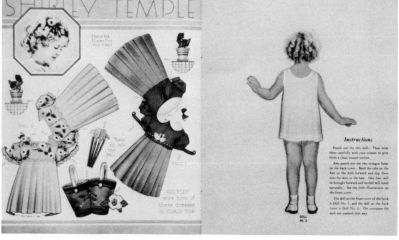

#1715 Reverse side of back cover and last page of clothes.

Courtesy of Audrey Sepponen.

1733 *MY TWINS* (Originated from a foreign book.) $2.00

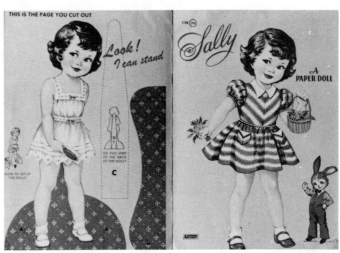

Courtesy of Emma Terry.

1734 *SALLY* (Originated from a foreign book.) $2.00

Courtesy of Audrey Sepponen.

1735 *ANNE* (Originated from a foreign book.) $2.00

Courtesy of Betsy Slap.

1736 *HELEN* (Originated from a foreign book.) $2.00

Courtesy of Shirley Hedge.

1739 *SHIRLEY TEMPLE PLAYHOUSE* 1935 - Box. $50.00 & up.

1739 Doll of Shirley, her doll carriage and one page of clothes from The Playhouse set.

Courtesy of Emma Terry.

1761 *SHIRLEY TEMPLE DOLLS AND DRESSES* 1937. $50.00 & up.

Courtesy of Marge Meisinger.

1782 *SHIRLEY TEMPLE* 1939. $60.00 & up.

Courtesy of Saalfield Archives.

1765 *SHIRLEY TEMPLE* 1936. 34" High. $75.00 & up.

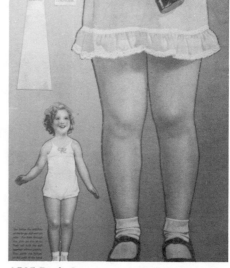

1765 Back Cover

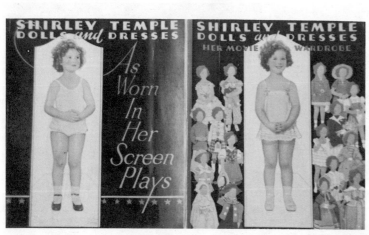

Courtesy of Saalfield Archives.

1773 *SHIRLEY TEMPLE - HER MOVIE WARDROBE* 1938. $60.00 & up.

Courtesy of Marge Meisinger.

1787 *SHIRLEY TEMPLE - IN MASQUERADE COSTUMES* 1940. $50.00 & up.

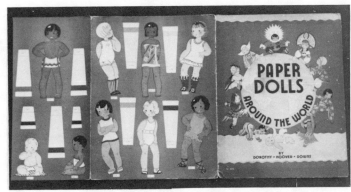

1954 *BABY DOLLS* 1941. $6.00

2106 *PAPER DOLLS AROUND THE WORLD* 1935. $10.00

2097 *COMICS PAPER DOLL CUT-OUT BOOK* 1935. Copyright **King Features Syndicate Inc. Courtesy of Saalfield Archives. $75.00 & up.**

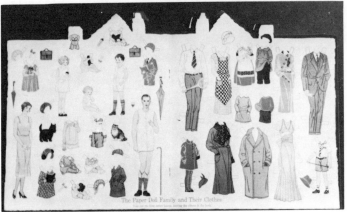

2094 *PAPER DOLL FAMILY AND THEIR HOUSE* 1934. $30.00

#2094 Inside center pages.

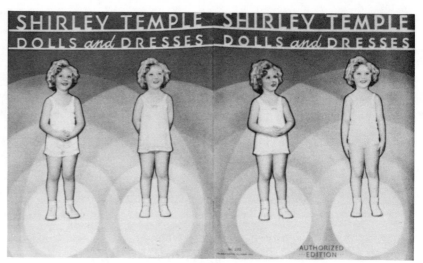

2109 *PAPER DOLL FAMILY* 1935. $25.00

2112 *SHIRLEY TEMPLE - DOLLS AND DRESSES* 1934. $50.00

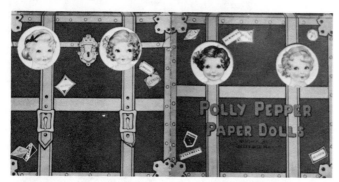

Courtesy of Saalfield Archives.

2126 *POLLY PEPPER PAPER DOLLS* 1936.
$25.00

#2126 A picture of the four dolls.

2140 *HOUSEKEEPING WITH THE KUDDLE KIDDIES* 1936.
$20.00

2131 *SCOOTLES AND KEWPIE DOLL BOOK* 1936. $60.00 & up.

Courtesy of Grayce Piemontesi.

Courtesy of Betsy Slap.

2176 *LET'S PLAY DOCTOR* 1938. $25.00

2160 *PETUNIA AND PAT-CHES* 1937. $30.00

Courtesy of Betsy Slap.

#2176 Inside page of dolls.

2164 *DRESSES WORN BY THE "FIRST LADIES" OF THE WHITE HOUSE* 1937. $35.00

2183 *KITCHEN PLAY* (with paper dolls) 1938. $10.00

#2183 Inside first page.

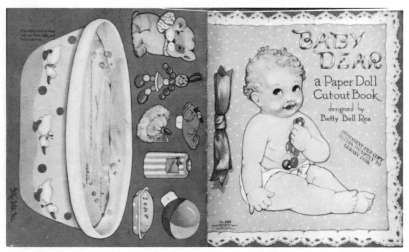

Courtesy of Saalfield Archives.

2185 *BABY DEAR* 1938. $25.00

Courtesy of Saalfield Archives.

2193 *FASHION SHOP* 1938. $25.00

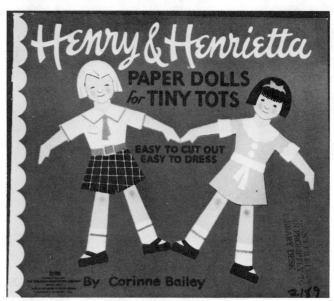

2189 *HENRY AND HENRIETTA* 1938. $20.00

#2193 Inside page of dolls.

2194 *LET'S PLAY WEDDING* 1938. $30.00

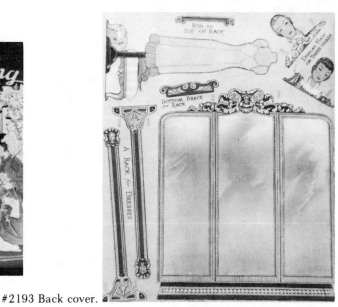

#2193 Back cover.

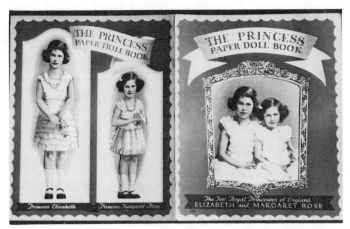

2216 *THE PRINCESS PAPER DOLL BOOK* 1939. $55.00

C2231 *THE NEW ZOO REVUE* 1974. Paper dolls of Henrietta Hippo, Freddie and Charlie with costumes to be colored. $3.00

2284 *RUTH E. NEWTON'S PAPER DOLL CUT-OUTS* 1940. $30.00

2245 *GOLDILOCKS AND THE THREE BEARS* 1939. $30.00

2242 *HOLLYWOOD FASHION DOLLS* 1939. $10.00

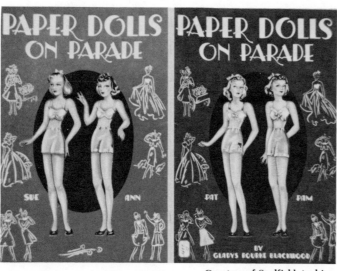

Courtesy of Audrey Sepponen.

2313 *50 PAPER DOLLS* 1940. $20.00

Courtesy of Saalfield Archives.

2295 *PAPER DOLLS ON PARADE* 1940. $15.00

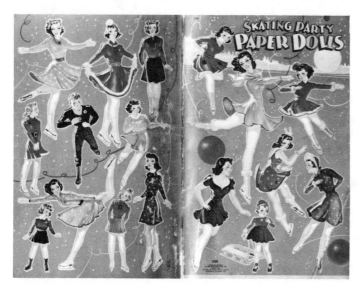

2328 *SKATING PARTY PAPER DOLLS* 1941. $10.00

Courtesy of Saalfield Archives.

2329 *14 GOOD LITTLE DOLLS* 1941. $15.00

Courtesy of Saalfield Archives.

2335 *CHILDREN OF AMERICA* 1941. (Coloring/paper doll book.) $10.00

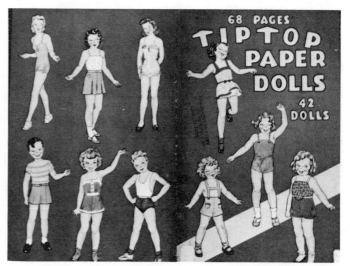

Courtesy of Saalfield Archives.

2321 *TIPTOP PAPER DOLLS* 1940. $20.00

Courtesy of Grayce Piemontesi.

2348 *THE BADGETT QUADRUPLETS* 1941. $40.00

#2348 Inside front cover.

Courtesy of Emma Terry.

2356 *CHARLIE CHAPLIN AND PAULETTE GODDARD* 1941.
$75.00 & up.

2358 *LITTLE MISS AMERICA* 1941. $20.00

2360 *DAISY MAE AND LI'L ABNER* 1941. $20.00

2361 *DEBS AND SUB DEBS* 1941. $10.00

Copyright United Feature Syndicate. Courtesy of Audrey Sepponen.

Courtesy of Saalfield Archives.

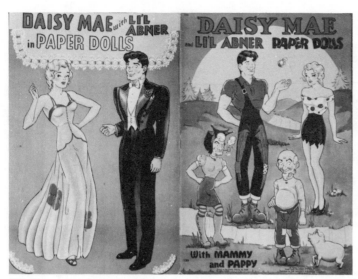

#2389   Copyright United Feature Syndicate. Courtesy of Audrey Sepponen.   #2397

#2400

#2408

2389 *DAISY MAE AND LI'L ABNER* 1942. $20.00

2397 *THE MODERN MISS IN PAPER DOLLS* 1942. $10.00

2400 *SCHOOL GIRL* 1942. $15.00

2408 *JANE ARDEN* 1942. $30.00

2410 *PAPER DOLL PARTY* 1944. According to Saalfield records, this book was completed in 1941. The copyright date on the book is 1944. In the three years between there were box sets using these dolls and a jobber book (#279) in 1943. No explanation is given for the three year wait. Maybe the date on the book was misprinted or it was decided to bring this original book out at a later date. $10.00

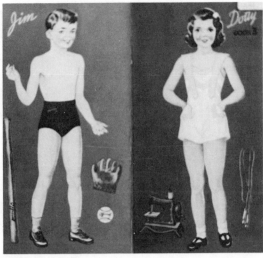

#2421 - Book 3.

Courtesy of Saalfield Archives. #2421 - Books 1 and 2.
2421 3 PAPER DOLL BOOKS 1942 (in a partial box). $15.00

2424 MOMMY AND ME 1943. $15.00

Courtesy of Emma Terry.

2425 THE NEW SHIRLEY TEMPLE IN PAPER DOLLS
1942. $40.00

Courtesy of Norene McDonald.

2427 MARY MARTIN 1942. $45.00

Courtesy of Emma Terry.

2426 JOAN CARROLL 1942. $25.00

Courtesy of Virginia Crossley.

2430 *QUIZ KIDS* 1942. $25.00

Courtesy of Saalfield Archives.

2431 *FESTIVAL PAPER DOLLS* 1944. $15.00

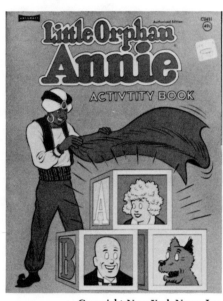

Copyright New York News, Inc.

C2431 *LITTLE ORPHAN ANNIE ACTIVITY BOOK* 1974. $2.00

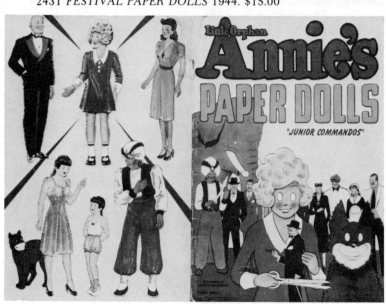

Courtesy of Shirley Hedge.

2436 *LITTLE ORPHAN ANNIE'S PAPER DOLLS* 1943. "Junior Commandos". $40.00

Copyright New Zoo Revue Joint Venture.

2438 *ANN SOTHERN* 1943. $40.00

Courtesy of Audrey Sepponen.

C2432 *NEW ZOO REVUE ACTIVITY BOOK* 1974. $2.00

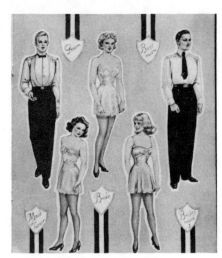

#2446 Inside front cover.

Courtesy of Audrey Sepponen.

2446 *ARMY AND NAVY WEDDING PARTY* 1943. $20.00

Courtesy of Shirley Hedge.

2445 *VICTORY PAPER DOLLS* 1943. $15.00

Courtesy of Betsy Slap.

2450 *UNCLE SAM'S LITTLE HELPERS* 1943. $25.00

Courtesy of Emma Terry.

2451 *CLAUDETTE COLBERT* 1943. $45.00

Courtesy of Emma Terry.

2458 *SWEETHEART PAPER DOLLS* 1943. $15.00

Courtesy of Audrey Sepponen.

2460 *BOOTS AND HER BUDDIES* 1943. $25.00

2462 *BETTY FIELD* 1943. $25.00

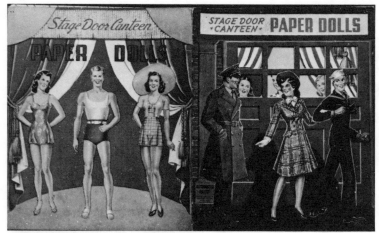

2468 *STAGE DOOR CANTEEN*
1943. $15.00

#2468 Inside front cover.

2478 *NANCY AND HER DOLLS*
1944. $10.00

Courtesy of Emma Terry.

2475 *LUCILLE BALL* 1944. $40.00

2481 *HOUR OF CHARM* 1943. $25.00

#2481 Inside front cover.

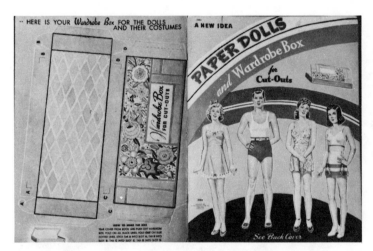

2484 *PAPER DOLLS AND WARDROBE BOX* 1944. $12.00

C2484 *SPACE 1999* (Cut and color book, with one paper doll) 1975. $1.00

Copyright ATV Licensing Ltd.

2485 *ROCK-A-BYE BABY* 1945. $8.00

Courtesy of Saalfield Archives.

2486 *BOB AND BETTY* 1945. $15.00

2487 *GOOD NEIGHBOR* 1944. $10.00

#2487 Inside page.

#2488 Inside front cover.

2488 *CARNIVAL* 1944. $10.00   **Courtesy of Emma Terry.**

2489 *ARTIST MODELS* 1945. $10.00

Courtesy of Saalfield Archives.

2497 *RAGGEDY ANN AND ANDY* 1944. $15.00

2492 *MARY MARTIN* 1944. $35.00

Courtesy of Audrey Sepponen.

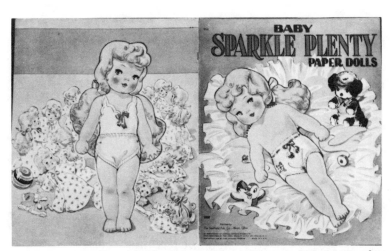

Copyright The Chicago Tribune. Courtesy of Virginia Crossley.

Box cover of #5160.

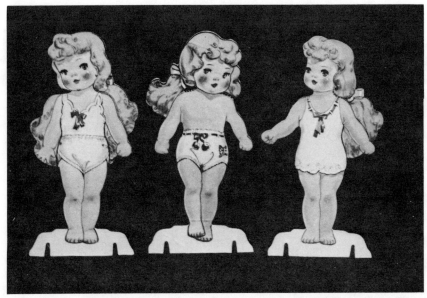

fig. #1   fig. #2   fig. #3

2500 *BABY SPARKLE PLENTY* 1948. The book of Baby Sparkle Plenty #2500 and the box set #5160 were produced at the same time. Because the book only used two of the three dolls used in the box, both will be pictured here. A soft cover jobber book (not pictured) was also published in 1948 and is #1510. The dolls in the box set are of heavy cardboard and are pictured below. The book #2500 used the dolls of fig. #1 and #2. The book #1510 used the dolls of fig. #2 and #3. The doll figures in the books were reversed from the dolls in the box, but it made no difference in the fit of the outfits which were the same for all three sets. Book - $12.00; Box - $15.00.

2503 *CLAUDETTE COLBERT* 1945. $35.00

Courtesy of Saalfield Archives.

2518 *ROMANCE PAPER DOLLS* 1945. $8.00

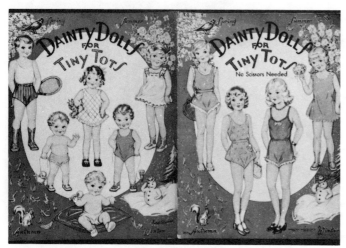

2519 *DAINTY DOLLS FOR TINY TOTS* 1946. $8.00

2520 *PUSH-OUT PAPER DOLLS* 1946. $8.00

2546 *AIR HOSTESS* 1947. $12.00

Courtesy of Saalfield Archives.

Courtesy of Audrey Sepponen.

2550 *SCHOOLMATES* 1947. $8.00

2564 *FAMILY OF PAPER DOLLS* 1947. $10.00

2576 *HONEY KITTEN* 1948. $8.00

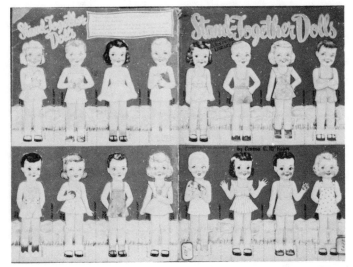

Courtesy of Saalfield Company Library.

2583 *STAND TOGETHER PAPER DOLLS* 1947. $6.00

2584 *16 PAPER DOLLS* 1948. $10.00

2590 *CINDERELLA* 1950. $15.00

Courtesy of Saalfield Archives.

2598 *ANIMAL PAPER DOLLS* 1950. $12.00

2600 *HEDY LAMARR* 1951. $25.00

2604 *DORA GROWS UP* 1951. $5.00

2605 *GIGI PERREAU* 1951. $15.00

2608 *SWEETHEART PAPER DOLLS* 1951. $7.00

Courtesy of Saalfield Archives.

2610 *CIRCUS* 1952. $8.00

Courtesy of Saalfield Archives.

2611 *WINTER GIRL WENDY, SUMMER GIRL SUE* 1952. $10.00

2612 *PALS AND PETS* 1952. $10.00

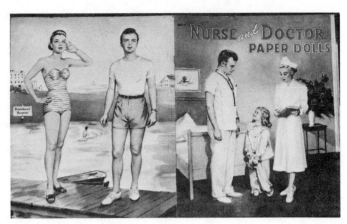

2613 *NURSE AND DOCTOR* 1952. $10.00

Courtesy of Saalfield Company Library.

2614 *PICNIC* 1952. $10.00

Courtesy of Saalfield Archives.

2615 *HAPPY BIRTHDAY* 1952. $8.00

Courtesy of Saalfield Archives.

2616 *BALLET PAPER DOLLS* 1953. $8.00

2617 *MERRY TEENS* 1953. $5.00

Courtesy of Saalfield Archives.

2618 *SOUTHERN BELLES* 1953. $6.00

Courtesy of Saalfield Archives.

2619 *BEST FRIENDS* 1953. $10.00

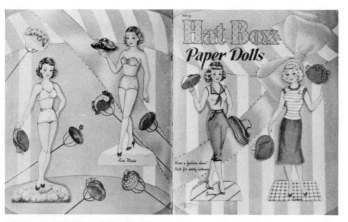

2620 *HAT BOX* 1954. $8.00

Courtesy of Audrey Sepponen.

2621 *PERT AND PRETTY* 1954. $6.00

Courtesy of Saalfield Company Library.

2622 *TOWN AND COUNTRY* 1954. $10.00

Courtesy of Saalfield Archives.

2700 *DOLL HOUSE PAPER DOLLS* 1948. $10.00

Courtesy of Saalfield Company Library.

2701 *TEEN SHOP* 1948. $6.00

Courtesy of Emma Terry.

2706 *PRINCE AND PRINCESS* 1949. $10.00

Courtesy of Saalfield Archives.

2709 *DELUXE MOUNTED DOLLS WITH DRESSES* 1949. $10.00

2708 *4 GREAT BIG PAPER DOLLS* 1949. $10.00
#2708 was not available, its reprint #4330 is pictured.

Courtesy of Emma Terry

2712 *CARMEN PAPER DOLLS - RITA HAYWORTH* 1948. $20.00

Courtesy of Bob Kelly.

2713 *PASTING WITHOUT PASTE - LITTLE DRESSMAKERS* 1949. $10.00

2715 *PASTING WITHOUT PASTE PAPER DOLLS - FOR LITTLE DRESSMAKERS* 1950. $10.00

Courtesy of Audrey Sepponen.

2717 *DUTCH TREAT* 1961. $4.00

2716 *RIDERS OF THE WEST* 1950. $10.00

#2716 Inside front cover.

#2717 Inside front cover.

2717 *SQUARE DANCE* 1950. $10.00

2718 *BRAND NEW BABY* 1951. $6.00

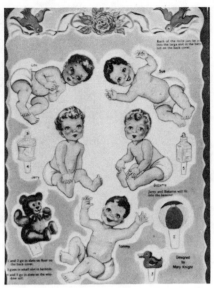

#2718 Inside front cover.

2721 *WEDDING PARTY* 1951. $10.00

Courtesy of Norene McDonald.

2722 *FAYE EMERSON* 1952. $15.00

2723 *CARMEN MIRANDA* 1952. $25.00

Copyright The Chicago Tribune. Courtesy of Betsy Slap.

2724 *BONNY BRAIDS* 1951. $15.00

Courtesy of Audrey Sepponen.
2725 JOAN CAULFIELD 1953. $15.00-20.00.

2730 CALICO CUT-OUTS 1953. $6.00

2731 LARAINE DAY 1953. $15.00-20.00.

2732 DIANA LYNN 1953. $15.00-20.00.

Copyright Judy Holliday.
2734 PENNY AND HER PETS (Originated from a foreign book.)
$4.00

Courtesy of Audrey Sepponen.
2733 LINDA DARNELL 1953. $15.00-20.00.

2734 *JUDY HOLLIDAY.* $15.00-20.00

Copyright Hal Roach Jr. and Roland Reid Television Productions, Inc.
2735 *JUNE AND STU ERWIN* 1954. $15.00-20.00.

2735 *SANDY* (Originated from a foreign book.) $4.00

Courtesy of Audrey Sepponen.
2736 *LITTLE TODDLERS* 1954. $8.00

Copyright Rovan Films. Courtesy of Emma Terry.
2737 *MY LITTLE MARGIE* 1954. (Gale Storm). $15.00-20.00.

Courtesy of Audrey Sepponen.
2738 *PAPER DOLL PATSY AND HER PALS* 1954. $10.00

Courtesy of Audrey Sepponen.

2739 *PAPER DOLLS WITH GLAMOUR GOWNS* 1954. $8.00

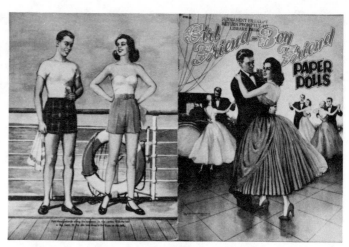

2740 *GIRL FRIEND-BOY FRIEND* 1954. $8.00

2742 *BEAUTY QUEEN* No date. $7.00.

2743 *PAPER DOLL PLAYMATES* 1955. $5.00

2747 *BABY SITTER* 1956. $7.00

Courtesy of Audrey Sepponen.

2748 *ROBIN HOOD AND MAID MARIAN* 1956. $12.00

Courtesy of Emma Terry

2749 *BRIDAL PARTY* 1956. $7.00

Courtesy of Emma Terry.

2753 *CHARMING PAPER DOLLS* 1957. $5.00

Copyright Field Enterprises, Inc. Courtesy of Audrey Sepponen.

2755 *ANGEL PAPER DOLLS* 1957. $12.00

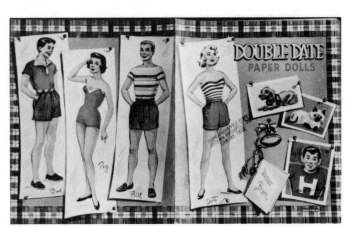

2757 *DOUBLE DATE* 1957. $5.00

2758 *PAPER DOLLS FROM MOTHER GOOSE* 1957. $5.00

Copyright California National Productions, Inc. Courtesy of Emma Terry.

2759 *LITTLE RASCALS - SPANKY AND DARLA* 1957. $15.00

Courtesy of Audrey Sepponen.

2760 *MAJORETTE PAPER DOLLS* 1957. $6.00

2761 *THE STORY PRINCESS* 1957. $18.00

Courtesy of Emma Terry.

2763 *ICE FESTIVAL* 1957. $6.00

2764 *A DAY WITH DIANE* 1957. $5.00

2765 *THE PETTICOAT GIRLS AND THEIR PARTY DRESSES* 1957. $5.00

2766 *FASHIONS FOR THE MODERN MISS* 1957. $5.00

Courtesy of Audrey Sepponen.

2767 *AROUND THE WORLD WITH CONNIE AND JEAN* 1958. $4.00

2779 *LILAC TIME* 1959. $5.00

Courtesy of Audrey Sepponen.

Courtesy of Audrey Sepponen.

2780 *SUGAR AND SPICE* 1959. $4.00

2783 *BABY BROTHER* 1959. $5.00

2798 *STORYLAND PAPER DOLLS.* $5.00

2882 *HERE COMES THE BRIDE* - Box 1949. $5.00

2883 *BABS* - Box 1949. $5.00

2884 *PEGGY* - Box 1949. $5.00

2885 *SALLY* - Box 1949. $5.00

Copyright New Zoo Revue Joint Venture.
N4042 *FOR MISS AMERICA - HENRIETTA HIPPO* 1974. $3.00

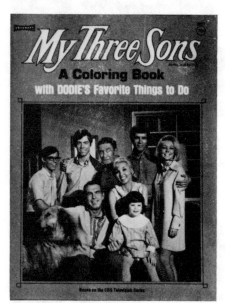

Copyright Columbia Broadcasting System, Inc.
3927 *MY THREE SONS* - Coloring and paper doll book. 1971.
$2.00

P4041 *DADDY'S GIRL* 1974. $2.00

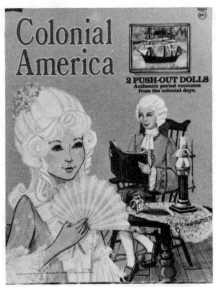

#N4043 Two inside pages showing dolls.

N4043 *COLONIAL AMERICA* 1974. $3.00

#R4113 Picture from 1976 catalog.

R4113 5 *LITTLE BELLES* - Box. $2.00

R4112 *SHORT STOP SUE AND HER WARDROBE* 1975 - Box.
$2.00

4187 *HEIDI AND PETER* 1957 - Box. $6.00

#4187 Dolls and one page of clothes.

#4186

#4211

#4213   Copyright 20th Century Fox Corp.

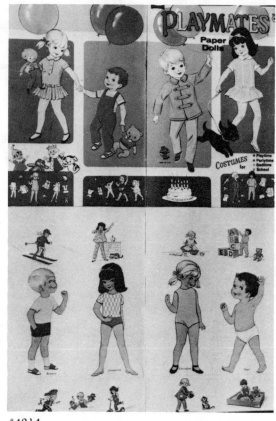

#4214

4186 *MY BONNIE LASSIE* 1957 - Box. $5.00

4211 *GOLDILOCKS AND THE THREE BEARS* 1970. $4.00

4213 *NANNY AND THE PROFESSOR* 1970. $5.00

4214 *PLAYMATES* (Originated from a foreign book.) $2.00

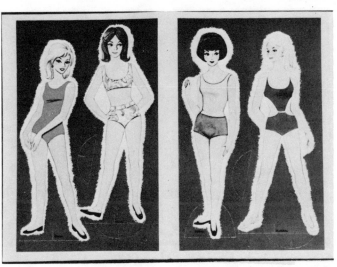

4217 *SHAMROCK PAPER DOLLS* (Originated from a foreign book.) $2.00

#4217 Inside covers with dolls.

4230 *MARY, MARY QUITE CONTRARY* 1972. $2.00

Copyright Columbia Pictures Industries, Inc.

4218 *SUSAN DEY* 1972. $5.00

4231 *AMY JO PAPER DOLLS* 1972. $2.00

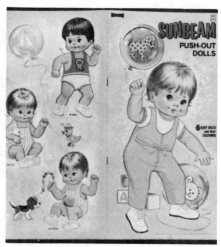

4232 *HOLLY, A COSTUME PAPER DOLL* 1972. $2.00

4233 *BALLET PAPER DOLL* 1972. $2.00

4235 *SUNBEAM* 1974. $1.00

4236 *PRINTS AND POLKA DOTS* 1973. $1.00

4248 *TRICIA PAPER DOLL* 1970. $5.00

4260 *TEEN BOUTIQUE* 1973. $1.00

4262 *FAVE TEENS* 1973.
$1.00

4263 *GIRLFRIENDS* 1973.
$1.00

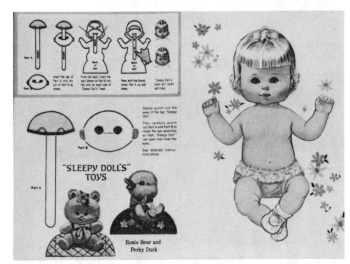

4280 *SLEEPY DOLL* 1971. $3.00

#4280 Inside front and back covers.

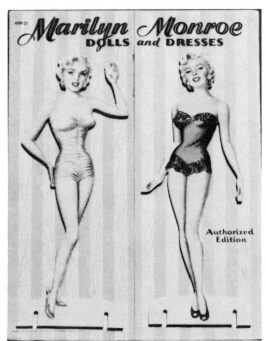

Courtesy of Emma Terry.

4308 *MARILYN MONROE* 1953. $50.00

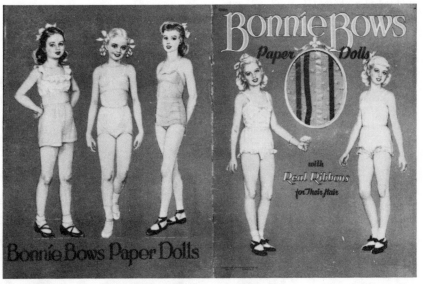

4309 *BONNIE BOWS* 1953. $5.00

4310 *EVE ARDEN* 1953. $25.00

#4310 Inside front cover.

#4310 Inside back cover.

Courtesy of Audrey Sepponen.

#4311 Inside front cover.

#4311 Inside back cover.

4311 *ARLENE DAHL* 1953. $25.00

Copyright Barbara Britton. Courtesy of Audrey Sepponen.

#4318 Inside front cover.

#4318 Inside back cover.

4318 *BARBARA BRITTON* 1954. $25.00

4312 *CORONATION PAPER DOLLS AND COLORING BOOK* 1953. $15.00

Copyright Rhonda Fleming. Courtesy of Audrey Sepponen.

4320 *RHONDA FLEMING* 1954. Paper dolls and coloring book. $25.00

Copyright Ozzie Nelson. Courtesy of Audrey Sepponen.

4319 *OZZIE AND HARRIET* 1954. $20.00

#4319 Inside front cover.

#4319 Inside back cover.

4321 *PRINCE VALIANT AND PRINCESS ALETA* 1954. $15.00

#4321   Copyright King Features Syndicate, Inc.

Copyright King Features Syndicate, Inc.

4326 *JULIET JONES PAPER DOLLS AND COLORING BOOK* 1955. $20.00

Copyright Russ-Field Corp. Courtesy of Emma Terry.

4328 *JANE RUSSELL PAPER DOLLS AND COLORING BOOK* 1955. $20.00-25.00

Copyright American Broadcasting Co., Inc.

4343 *CURIOSITY SHOP* 1971. $2.00

Copyright Lewislor Films, Inc. Courtesy of Emma Terry.

4352 *LORETTA YOUNG PAPER DOLLS AND COLORING BOOK* 1956. $25.00

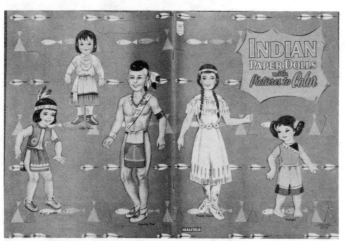

Copyright Audrey Sepponen.

4406 *INDIAN PAPER DOLLS WITH PICTURES TO COLOR* 1956. $5.00

Copyright of Ann Sothern. Courtesy of Emma Terry.

4407 *ANN SOTHERN* 1956. $20.00-25.00

Courtesy of Virginia Crossley.

4408 *MARDI GRAS* - King and Queen Statuette Dolls. 1956. $8.00

Copyright Columbia Pictures Corp. Courtesy of Audrey Sepponen.

4409 *KIM NOVAK PAPER DOLLS WITH PICTURES TO COLOR* 1957. $20.00-25.00

Courtesy of Audrey Sepponen.

4410 *LITTLE MISS ALICE PAPER DOLLS - PICTURES TO COLOR* 1957. $8.00

Courtesy of Audrey Sepponen.

4411 *IN OLD NEW YORK - COLONIAL PAPER DOLLS WITH PICTURES TO COLOR* 1957. $10.00

Copyright Screen Gems, Inc.

4412 *DONNA REED* 1959. $15.00

4413 *SANDRA DEE* 1959. $15.00

Copyright Universal Pictures Co. Inc.

4415 *SALLY TWINKLETOES AND PEGGY TWIRL* 1966. $3.00

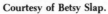

4414 *BABY DEARS* 1959. $5.00

Courtesy of Betsy Slap.

4420

#4420

4420 *HERE COMES THE BRIDE* 1967. $5.00

#4420 Inside front and back covers of Here Comes the Bride.

4416 *TOODLES THE TODDLER A WALKING PAPER DOLL* 1966. $3.00

Courtesy of Emma Terry.

4420 *SHEREE NORTH* 1957. $15.00

Copyright MLM Enterprises, Inc. Courtesy of Audrey Sepponen.

4421 *GISELLE MAC KENZIE* 1957. $15.00

Courtesy of Audrey Sepponen.

4422 *VIRGINIA MAYO* 1957. $15.00

Copyright Universal Pictures Co., Inc.

4423 *MARTHA HYER* 1958. $15.00

4424 *JULIE ANDREWS* 1958. $15.00

Copyright Evelyn Rudie.

4425 *EVELYN RUDIE* 1958. $10.00

Copyright MLM Enterprises, Inc. Courtesy of Audrey Sepponen
4428 *GISELLE MAC KENZIE* 1958. $15.00-20.00

4430   *CAMPUS SWEET-HEARTS* 1957. (A carry-doll kit). $5.00

4430 *KIDDIE CIRCUS* 4.00

Courtesy of Audrey Sepponen.

Copyright Columbia Pictures Corp. Courtesy of Emma Terry.
4429   *KIM   NOVAK*   1958.
$25.00

4431 *FLOWER GIRLS* 1957.
(A carry-doll kit). $5.00

Courtesy of Bob Kelly.

4431 *BALLET PAPER DOLLS* A Double Doll Book 1964. $5.00

4431 *BONNETS AND BOWS.* $5.00

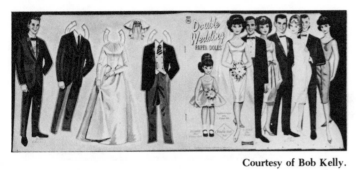

4432 *DOUBLE WEDDING* A Double Doll Book 1964. $5.00

4432 *TUESDAY WELD* 1960. $15.00

4433 *TAMMY MARIHUGH* 1960. $15.00

4433 *UNITED NATIONS* A Double Doll Book 1964. $5.00

4434 *BLONDIE* 1968. $5.00

#4434 Inside back and front covers.

Copyright K.A.M. Productions Corp.

4434 *POLLY BERGEN* 1958. $15.00-20.00

4436 *FINIAN'S RAINBOW* 1968. $5.00

#4436 Outside front and back covers at top. Inside front and back cover at bottom. **Copyright Warner Bros. - Seven Arts, Inc. Courtesy of Virginia Crossley.**

Courtesy of Bob Kelly. Front and back of folder and dolls.

4435 *SHIRLEY TEMPLE* 1958. $15.00

Courtesy of Virginia Crossley.

4435 *JULIA* 1968. $8.00

#4435 Inside front and back covers.

Copyright The Chicago Tribune - News Syndicate, Inc.

4438 *BRENDA STARR* 1964. $15.00

Courtesy of Virginia Crossley.

4439 *JUDY DOLL - MISS TEENAGE AMERICA* 1964. $10.00

Copyright American Broadcasting - Paramount Theatres, Inc. Courtesy of Virginia Crossley.

4440 *HOOTENANNY* 1964. $8.00

#4440 Inside front cover of Hootenanny.

4440 *MINI MOPPETS* 1969. $2.00

4441 *MINI MODS* 1969. $2.00

4442 *SUGAR AND SPICE* 1969. $2.00

Courtesy of Pam Hunter.

4441 *JOANNE WOODWARD* 1958. $15.00-20.00

#4441 Outside covers of folder at top. Dolls and one page of clothes at bottom.

4443 *DOLLY AND ME* 1969. $2.00

Courtesy of Pam Hunter.

4444 *THE OLD WOMAN WHO LIVED IN A SHOE* 1960. $8.00

#4444 Inside front cover.

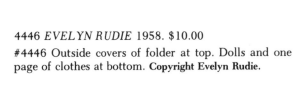

#4446

4445 *LITTLE WOMEN* 1960. $10.00

4446 *EVELYN RUDIE* 1958. $10.00

#4446 Outside covers of folder at top. Dolls and one page of clothes at bottom. **Copyright Evelyn Rudie.**

#4445 Inside front and back covers.

4448 *TEXAS ROSE* 1959 (date from Saalfield records). $10.00

4449 *THROUGH THE YEAR WITH CINDY* 1959. $5.00

Copyright California National Productions, Inc.

4447 *SHARI LEWIS* 1958. $15.00

4452 *SUGAR PLUM PALS*
1966. $5.00

4451 *PAPER DOLL PLAYMATES*
1966. $5.00

#4452 Inside front and back covers.

#4451 Inside front and back covers.

4475 *WHITE HOUSE PAPER DOLLS* 1969. $5.00

4479 *THAT GIRL - STARRING - MARLO THOMAS* 1967. $6.00

4469 *MOD FASHIONS - FEATURING JANE FONDA* 1966. $8.00

Copyright Daisy Production, Inc.

#4469

#4469 Inside front cover.

#4469 Inside back cover.

Courtesy of Bob Kelly.

4486 *WIGGIE THE MOD MODEL* 1967. $4.00

#4486 Inside front cover. Pocket on reverse side of front cover for outfits.

Copyright Walt Disney Productions. Courtesy of Virginia Crossley.

#4487 Inside front cover.

#4487 Inside back cover.

4487 *THE HAPPIEST MILLIONAIRE* 1967. $6.00

Copyright Jos. L. Kallus.

#4488 Inside front and back cover.

4488 *KEWPIE KIN* 1967. $8.00

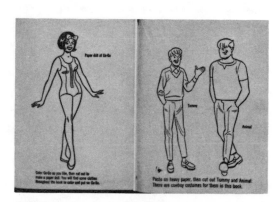

4612 *TIPPY TEEN COLORING BOOK AND PAPER DOLLS*
1967. $3.00. #4612 not available, pictured is its reprint #4512.

#4612 Inside pages of dolls.

5113 *CLASSIC BOUTIQUE* (Originated from a foreign book.) $2.00

5110 *SHIRLEY TEMPLE* 1958. 18" Doll folds to fit in pocket of folder. $20.00

5111 *THE CANDY STRIPERS* 1973. $3.00

#5111 Inside front and back covers.

Copyright Columbia Pictures Industries, Inc.

#5112 Inside front and back covers.

5112 *LOST HORIZON* 1973. $4.00

Copyright Columbia Broadcasting System, Inc.

5115 *DODIE - FROM "MY THREE SONS"* 1971. $4.00

#5115 Inside front and back covers.

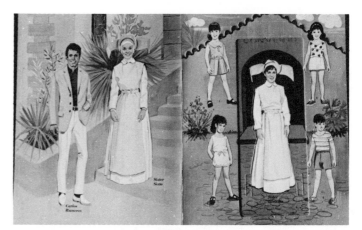

Copyright Screen Gems, Inc.

5121 *THE FLYING NUN* 1968. $6.00

#5121 Inside front and back covers.

Copyright Columbia Pictures Industries, Inc.

5137 *THE PARTRIDGE FAMILY* 1971. $4.00

#5137 Inside front and back covers.

Copyright Columbia Broadcasting System, Inc.

5139 *HEE HAW* 1971. $4.00

#5139 Inside front and back cover.

Courtesy of Saalfield Archives.
5180 *JEANNETTE* 1954 - Box. $5.00

Courtesy of Saalfield Archives.
5181 *CORINNE* 1954 - box. $5.00

Courtesy Betsy Slap.

5214 *CRADLE BABY* 1948. Baby fits in cradle on front cover. Outfits are inside book. $10.00

Copyright Osbro Productions, Inc.

5225 *MARIE OSMOND* 1973. $6.00

#5225 Inside front and back covers.

5229 *LITTLE GIRLS ARE EVERYTHING NICE.* (Originated from a foreign book.) $3.00

#5229 Inside front and back covers.

Courtesy of Audrey Sepponen.

5215 *PAPOOSIE* 1949. Doll and storybook, no outfits. $8.00

5246 *SUMMERTIME SUE, WINTERTIME WENDY* 1974. $3.00

6020 *PRESCHOOL PAPER DOLLS* 1958 - Box. $5.00

Courtesy of Bob Kelly.

Courtesy of Marge Meisinger.

5326 *SHIRLEY TEMPLE BUSY BOOK* 1959. Included is a paper doll of Shirley's doll and outfits to be colored. $12.00

#6027

#6028   Courtesy of Bob Kelly.

#6041   Courtesy of Bob Kelly.

#6042   Copyright Harvey Famous Cartoons.

#6052

6027 *DARLING DOLLS WITH WAVY HAIR* 1952 - Box. $10.00

6028 *LOVELY DOLLS WITH REAL CLOTH DRESSES* 1952 - Box. $10.00

6052 *SWEETHEART DOLLS* 1954 - Box. $10.00

6041 *MARY LOU - A DARLING DOLL WITH WAVY HAIR* 1958 - Box. $5.00

6042 *LITTLE AUDREY'S DRESS DESIGNERS KIT* 1962 - Box. $15.00

6045 *LAUGH-IN PARTY* 1969 - Box. $10.00

Copyright George Schlatter, Ed Friendly Productions and Romart, Inc.

6054 *ELIZABETH THE BEAUTIFUL BRIDE* 1966 - Box. (Elizabeth is the daughter of Mr. Henry Saalfield.) $7.00

6054 *HAPPINESS IS LEARNING HOW* 1973 - Box. Activity box with weatherman paper doll. $3.00

Courtesy of 1973 Saalfield catalog.

Courtesy of Virginia Crossley. Copyright Lenore Niernberg and Betty Waserman.

6057 *FASHION WHIRL PAPER DOLLS* - Game 1968/70. $4.00

6058 *PATCHY ANNIE* The Rockaway Doll 1962 - Box. $4.00

6058 *THE HOLIDAY TWINS BETTY AND BOBBY* 1970 - Box. $3.00. Courtesy of Marilyn Johnson.

Courtesy of Bob Kelly.

6059 *PATCHWORK PAPER DOLLS* 1971 - Box. $3.00

6061 *MAKE BELIEVE AND PLAY STEWARDESS* 1970 - Box. $5.00

Copyright California National Productions, Inc.

6060 *SHARI LEWIS AND HER PUPPETS* 1960 - Box. $15.00

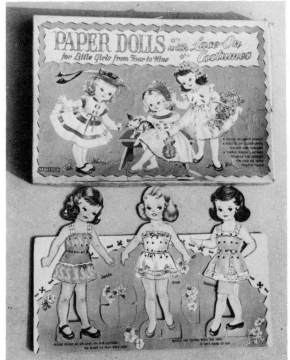

Janie, Sue and Nancy. **Courtesy of Edith Linn.**

#6068 Carol, Bunny and Linda at top. #6068 Michele, Carolyn and Elaine at bottom.

6068 *PAPER DOLLS WITH LACE-ON COSTUMES* - Carol, Bunny and Linda - Box. $3.00

6068 *PAPER DOLLS WITH LACE-ON COSTUMES* - Michele, Carolyn and Elaine - Box. $3.00

There were three different box sets of "Paper Dolls With Lace-On Costumes" #6068. The first was in 1955 with dolls of Janie, Sue and Nancy. The second set was done in the 1960's with dolls of Carol, Bunny and Linda. the third set had dolls of Michele, Carolyn and Elaine. This set was done in the late 1960's. All three sets were reprinted a number of times with new box covers in the years to follow.

6068 *PAPER DOLLS WITH LACE-ON COSTUMES* - Janie, Sue and Nancy 1955 - Box. $7.00

#6078

#6079

#6088   Copyright Jos. L. Kallus.

6078 *MOTHER AND DAUGHTER* 1963 - Box. $5.00

6079 *DARLING DOLLS WITH WAVY HAIR* 1957 - Box. $10.00

6088 *KEWPIE DOLLS* 1963 - Box. $15.00

6091 *PENNY* 1964 - Box. $5.00

6092 *CONNIE DARLING* And Her Dolly 1964 - Box. $5.00

#6092   #6091

#6092 Close-up of dolls Connie and her dolly.

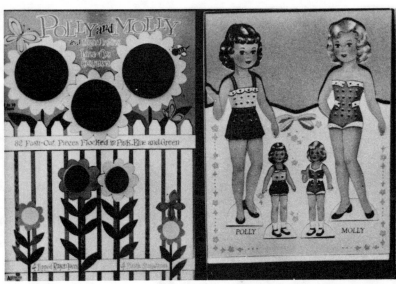

6116 *POLLY AND MOLLY AND THEIR DOLLIES* 1958 - Box. (This set was also issued with another box top design. Same number 6116). $7.00

6097 *SWEETHEART DOLLS* With Cloth Dresses 1957 - Box. $10.00

6093 *PAPER DOLL BALLET* 1957 - Box. $10.00

6128 *FOUR HI-HEEL STANDING DOLLS* - Magic Stay-on Costumes 1959 - Box. $10.00

6160 *YOU ARE A DOLL* - Box (Doll has a blank face for child's picture). $10.00

6117 *KATHY AND SUE* - Two "Just Like Me" Dolls 1958 - Box. $12.00

6169 *3 DARLING DOLLS* 1964 - Box. $7.00

6189 *6 STANDING DOLLS WITH LACE-ON COSTUMES* 1956 - Box. $10.00

6194 *DARLING DOLLS WITH WAVY HAIR*. Costumes with the velvet touch. 1957. $10.00

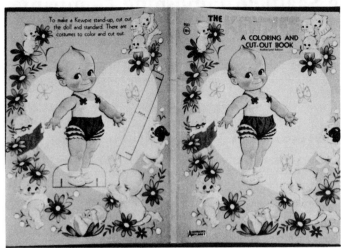

Copyright Jos. L. Kallus. Courtesy of Virginia Crossley.
9553 *THE KEWPIES* - A Coloring and Cut-Out Book 1962. $5.00

Courtesy of Emma Terry.
9568 *STORY OF THE BALLET* 1963/64. A coloring and paper doll book. (This book began as a coloring book in 1963 and paper dolls were added in 1964.) $4.00

Courtesy of Emma Terry. Showing the cover of the three part folder.
9859 *SHIRLEY TEMPLE PLAY KIT* 1958. $20.00

Courtesy of Emma Terry.
9619 *ONCE UPON A WEDDING DAY* Coloring and cut-out book. $4.00

#9859 Inside of the three part folder.

Courtesy of Jane Sugg.
JACK AND JILL COLORING BOOK 1915 - The Title Page reads NURSERY PAINTING BOOK. Contains one paper doll, outfit and hat to color.

Books Without Numbers

E DOLL BOOK - Four 12" dolls, listed in catalogs of the 1920's. Not available for picturing.

F DOLL BOOK - Four dolls, listed in catalogs of the 1920's. Not available for picturing.

THE KEWPIE KUTOUTS 1914 - Not available for picturing.

BABIES OF ALL NATIONS. 1908 (Muslin book).

List of Paper Dolls Published by the Saalfield Publishing Company

This list also includes Artcraft books of paper dolls, Artcraft being a division of The Saalfield Publishing Company. Compiled through the help of old Saalfield catalogs, private collections and the Saalfield archives at the Kent State Libraries, this list contains both original and reprint books. All reprint books listed will carry a number in parentheses following their titles indicating the original from which the reprint is derived. Brackets without any numbers enclosed after the title indicate a reprint where the original is not definitely known. When dates are not given, either the book had no date or the date has not been verified.

5	*BOY AND GIRL CUT-OUT DOLL BOOK*, (appeared in the 1937 Saalfield catalog) originally copyrighted 1932 by the Stecher Lithographic Company
TR40	*MY PEEK-A-BOO SHOW BOOK* - stage settings, not paper dolls
VP41	*LET'S PLAY CIRCUS* - circus settings, not paper dolls
100	*BETTINA AND HER PLAYMATE ROSALIE* (appeared in the 1931 Saalfield catalog) originally copyrighted by the Stecher Lithographic Company
112	*PAPER DOLLY COLORING BOOK* (2335)
113	*UNITED WE STAND* 1943
115	*STYLE SHOP* 1943 (2397)
116	*JUDY AND JOYCE* 1943 (2424)
128	*PATTY AND SUE* 1944 (2216)
129	*PAPER DOLL BABIES* 1944 (1954)
154	*PAPER DOLL PLAYMATES* 1940 (885)
155	*PAPER DOLLS AROUND THE WORLD* (2106)
156	*GLORIA JEAN* 1940 (1661)
165	*MODERN PAPER DOLLS* 1940 (2295)
167	*SCHOOL FRIENDS* 1940 (2313)
177	*SUPERMAN* cut-outs - stand-ups
185	*PLAY WITH PAPER DOLLS* 1941 (2329)
188	*PAPER DOLLY BOOK* 1941 (2126)
193	*GLORIA JEAN* (1664)
197	*HAPPY PAPER DOLLS* [ ]
199	*CHARLIE CHAPLIN AND PAULETTE GODDARD* (2356)
200	*PAPER DOLLS PAINTED FROM LIFE* 1941 (2358)
203	*UP TO DATE PAPER DOLLS* 1941 (2295)
203	*MARGARET* (from assortment 2-BS)
204	*ALICE* (from assortment 2-BS)
204	*TEN LITTLE NEIGHBORS* 1941 (885)
212	*THE BADGETT QUADRUPLETS* 1941 (2348)
215	*LI'L ABNER AND DAISY MAE* 1941 (2360)
S218	*DOLLIES TO PAINT, CUT-OUT AND DRESS* (1180) Some books have been found to contain an extra doll from (1171)
X218	*DOLLIES TO PAINT, CUT-OUT AND DRESS* 1918 (1180)
222	*COUNTRY CLUB* 1941 (2361)
223	*GLORIA JEAN* 1941 [ ]
227	*PAPER DOLLS OF ALL NATIONS* 1939 (2106)
229	*SEVEN STANDING DOLLS WITH WOODEN BASES* 1939 - Box (230)
230	*PAPER DOLLS TO CUT-OUT*, 10 dolls with dresses, hats and playthings 1932
230	*PAPER DOLLS TO CUT-OUT*, - same as above, but with a different cover and dated 1939 (pages in color and to be colored)
231	*PAPER DOLL BOX* - 10 dolls, 170 pieces - 1932 catalog [ ]
231	*POLLY PEPPER PAPER DOLLS* 1936 (2126)
232	*DOLL BOX* - 15 dolls, walls for nursery, 50 pieces of furnishings, 148 pieces for costumes - 1932 catalog [ ]
233	*FRONT AND BACK PAPER DOLL BOX* 1933 (976 and 977)
235	*PLAY BOX OF FARM CUT-OUTS* - stand-ups
236	*THE WHOLE FAMILY IN PAPER DOLLS* - Box - 1939 catalog [ ]
239	*POLLY PEPPER PAPER DOLLS* - Box (2126)
239	*PLAY BOX OF GROCERY STORE CUT-OUTS* - stand-ups
242	*BEAUTIFUL PAPER DOLLS* 1941 (2358)
244	*WILD WEST CUT-OUTS* - stand-ups
245	*ARMY CUT-OUTS* - stand-ups
246	*ARMY CUT-OUTS* - stand-ups
246	*CUT-OUT PLAY BOOK*, dolls and nursery - 1934 catalog [ ]
247	*FIREMEN CUT-OUTS* - Box - stand-ups
247	*PAPER DOLL CUT-OUTS* - 1934 catalog [ ]
248	*FIREMAN CUT-OUTS* - Box - stand-ups
249	*CUT-OUT BOATS* - Box - stand-ups
250	*CUT-OUT BOATS* - Box - stand-ups
250	*JUNIOR MISS* 1942 (2400)
253	*TWENTY STANDING DOLLS*, 180 pieces [ ]
254	*GLORIA JEAN* 1941 - Box (1666)
254	*KITCHEN PLAY BOX* - 1939 catalog [ ]
255	*PRINCESS PAPER DOLLS* - Box (2216)
256	*HENRY AND HENRIETTA* - Box (2189)
257	*FIVE PAPER DOLL BOOKS* Box (2242)
258	*PAPER DOLLS OF ALL NATIONS*, New York Worlds Fair Edition - Box (2106)
259	*PAPER DOLLS AND DRESSES* - Box 1940 (2242)
259	*PAPER DOLLS AT BEACHSIDE* - Box - 1941 catalog (2242)
266	*SKATING PAPER DOLLS* 1942 (2328)
268	*PAPER DOLLS ON PARADE* (2295)
268	*MARY ANN* 1932 (956)
269	*FOUR SISTERS PAPER DOLLS* 1943 (2358)
269	*MICKEY MOUSE AND MINNIE MOUSE* 1933 (980)
271	*HAPPY CHILDREN* 1942 (2329)
272	*FOUR PLAYMATES* 1941 (2126)

274	*PLAYTIME PAPER DOLLS* 1942 (885)
275	*BETTY JANE* 1934
278	*JANE ARDEN* 1942 (2408)
279	*THE PAPER DOLLS GIVE A PARTY* 1943. This book (a jobber book) was copyrighted before the original (2410)
280	*SIX SHIRLEY TEMPLE DOLLS* 1934/1935 (2112 and 1715)
280	*DAISY MAE AND LI'L ABNER* 1943 (2389)
282	*JUST LIKE MOTHER* 1943 (2424)
283	*THE NEW SHIRLEY TEMPLE* 1942 (2425)
284	*JOAN CARROLL* 1942 (2426)
287	*DAISY'S CUT-OUT DOLL BOOK* - Listed in catalogs of the 1920's
287	*MARY MARTIN* 1943 (2427)
290	*SHIRLEY TEMPLE* 1936 (1715)
294	*QUIZ KIDS* 1942 (2430)
294	*LITTLE MARY MIXUP AND HER FRIEND PEGGY* 1922
295	*PAPER DOLLS* - Rose, Ice, Cherry, Cotton, May and Harvest Queens 1944 (2431)
299	*LITTLE ORPHAN ANNIE* 1943 (2436)
300	*SCOOTLES AND KEWPIE DOLL BOOK* (2131)
300	*MODERN MISS* 1942 (2397)
301	*ANN SOTHERN* 1943 (2438)
303	*POLLY AND MOLLY IN FANCY DRESS* 1943 (1787 Shirley Temple)
303	*SHIRLEY TEMPLE* 1937 (1761)
304	*KELLY SISTERS* 1944 (1782 Shirley Temple)
306	*OUR PAPER DOLLS GO TO SCHOOL* 1947 (2550)
306	*SCHOOLMATES* (2550)
313	*AIR, LAND AND SEA PAPER DOLLS* 1943 (2445)
314	*MILITARY WEDDING* 1943 (2446)
315	*PAPER DOLL CUT-OUTS OF GULLIVERS TRAVELS* 1939 (1261)
321	*RED, WHITE AND BLUE* 1943 (2450)
322	*CLAUDETTE COLBERT* 1943 (2451)
322	*PIN UP GIRL* 1945 (2489)
324	*GOOD NEIGHBOR PAPER DOLLS* 1944 (2487)
325	*CARNIVAL PAPER DOLLS* 1943. This book (a jobber book) was copyrighted before the original (2488)
329	*LITTLE MISS AMERICA* 1941 (2358)
330	*BOOTS AND HER BUDDIES* 1943 (2460)
332	*BETTY FIELD* 1943 (2462)
338	*SHIRLEY TEMPLE* 1938 (1773)
338	*LUCILLE BALL* (2475)
345	*PAPER DOLLY FUN* 1944 (2478)
347	*STAGE DOOR CANTEEN* 1943 (2468)
348	*HOUR OF CHARM* 1943 (2481)
349	*PAPER DOLLS WE LOVE* 1940 (2295)
350	*SCHOOL GIRL PAPER DOLLS* 1942 (2400)
351	*14 GOOD LITTLE DOLLS* 1941 (2329)
355	*PIN-UP GIRL* 1945 (2489)
362	*TWENTY PAPER DOLLS* 1938 (885)
363	*PAPER DOLLS WITH COSTUMES OF 21 NATIONS* (2106)
367	*MARY MARTIN* 1942 (2427)
368	*MARY MARTIN* 1944 (2492)
368	*DOLLY DIMPLE* Listed in catalogs of the 1920's
368	*POLLY DOLLY* listed in catalogs of the 1920's
369	*FASHION SHOP PAPER DOLLS* 1938 (2193)
369	*RAGGEDY ANN PAPER DOLLS* 1944 (2497)
370	*LET'S PLAY WEDDING* (2194)
378	*CLAUDETTE COLBERT* 1943 (2451)
379	*VACATION DAYS* 1947 (2518)
379	*THE PRINCESS PAPER DOLLS* 1939 (2216)
380	*TEN HAPPY PAPER DOLLS* 1947 (2519)
381	*PLAYHOUSE PAPER DOLLS* 1947 (2520)
383	*TEN PAPER DOLLS* [ ]
387	*WORLD'S FAIR PAPER DOLLS* (2106)
388	*COWBOY AND INDIAN CUT-OUTS* 1945 - stand-ups
392	*LITTLE MISS AMERICA* (2358)
397	*HOLLYWOOD FASHION DOLLS* 1939 (2242)
399	*SHIRLEY TEMPLE* 1939 (1782)
423	*LIB AND MARY* 1941 - Box (2358)
429	*STANDING PAPER DOLLS JUNE AND MARIE* 1942 - Box [2410]
447	*JOAN CARROLL* 1942 - Box (2426)
448	*MARY MARTIN* 1942 - Box (2427)
449	*ANN SOTHERN* 1943 - Box (2438)
450	*THE NEW SHIRLEY TEMPLE PAPER DOLLS* 1943 -Box (2425)
451	*RAGGEDY ANN AND ANDY* (2497)
452	*CLAUDETTE COLBERT* 1943 - Box (2451)
453	*REALLY TRULY PAPER DOLLS* 1943 - Box of four books (2358)
453	*LITTLE MISS AMERICA* 1943 (2358)
458	*HENRY AND HENRIETTA* 1938 (2189)
494	*A BOXFUL OF PAPER DOLLS* - 5 books - 1934/44 catalog [ ]

503   *PAPER DOLLS TO DRESS* 1951 [   ]
552   Five Activity Books for girls in a box - *DOLLY JEAN, LET'S PLAY DOCTOR, THE TRAILER FAMILY, SUNNY-DALE FARM* and *THE GROCERY STORE* 1939/40 catalog
567   *KINDERGARTEN PAPER DOLLS* - Box 50 dolls [   ]
577   *ALICE, BETTY, CONNIE AND DORIS* 1941 - Box (2358)
584   *PERSONALITY PAPER DOLLS* - Box (2400)
592   *PAPER DOLLS IN UNIFORMS OF THE U.S.A.* - Box - (2445)
593   *JUNIOR VOLUNTEERS* - Box [2450]
610   Box of five activity books for girls *HAPPY HOURS FOR GIRLS* includes one paper doll book *FIVE PAPER DOLLS* which comes from (230)
711   *WESTERN PAPER DOLLS* (4448)
714   *TUESDAY WELD* (4432)
715   *TAMMY MARIHUGH* (4433)
716   *CARNIVAL KING AND QUEEN* (4408)
717   *TEXAS ROSE* (4448)
718   *SUE AND PAM* (2766)
719   *COLLEGE CHUMS* (4430 Campus Sweethearts)
720   *BABY BROTHER* (2783)
721   *PEGGY LOU THE CALENDAR GIRL* 1961 (4449)
735   *INDIAN PAPER DOLLS WITH PAPOOSE* lace up and yarn (4406)
735   *BONNIE LASSIE* - lace up doll [   ]
804   *MY BOOK OF PAPER DOLLS* (1171)
850   *STORYBOOK PAPER DOLLS* (4187)
851   *MARDI GRAS* (4408)
852   *WESTERN PAPER DOLLS* (4448)
853   *SHIRLEY TEMPLE* (4435)
854   *FLOWER GIRLS* (4431)
855   *CAMPUS QUEENS* (4430)
856   *ROBIN HOOD* (2748)
857   *LITTLE MISS ALICE* (4410)
858   *INDIAN PAPER DOLLS* (4406)
859   *DAINTY DOLLIES* (2780)
860   *PERT AND PRETTY* (2620 Hat Box)
861   *BONNIE LASSIE* (2765 Petticoat)
877   *DOLLY JEAN, HER PAPER DOLL HOUSE* furniture and clothes 1932
881   *MANY THINGS TO DO* 1932 (one paper doll included)
885   *PAPER DOLLS,* 10 dolls - 180 pieces to cut out 1932
895   *A HAPPY FAMILY OF PAPER DOLLS* 1932 (230)
898   *JOAN AND JUDY'S PAPER DOLL BOX* 1943 from the following books -*ARMY AND NAVY WEDDING PARTY* #2446, *SWEETHEART* #2458 and *STAGE DOOR CANTEEN* #2468.
900   *THE PATCHWORK POSTER BOOK OF MOTHER GOOSE* 1927 (cut-out and paste)
916   *THE CUTTING AND PASTING BOOK OF MOTHER GOOSE* 1927
936   *MY BOOK OF PAPER DOLLS* - Linentex book (1171)
956   *SALLY LOU* 1931
963   *PETER RABBIT* 1934 - stand-ups
964   *ALICE IN WONDERLAND* 1934 - stand-ups
971   *LET'S PLAY STORE* 1933 - stand-ups
973   *LUNA PARK PANARAMA BOOK* 1933 - stand-ups
974   *WILD WEST PANARAMA BOOK* 1933 - stand-ups
975   *HILLSIDE FARM* 1933 - stand-ups
976   *DONNY DOUBLE* 1933
977   *DOTTY DOUBLE* 1933
980   *MICKEY MOUSE AND MINNIE MOUSE*
982   *EIGHT AUTOS TO BUILD* - stand-ups
989   *THE MANGER SCENE* to set-up 1933 - stand-ups
994   *TEN PAPER DOLLS* 1933 (230)
1010 *PAM AND HER DOLLY* (6092)
1011 *PAPER DOLLS WITH LACE-ON COSTUMES* 1969 (6068) Box (Michele & Carolyn)
1025 *TWO PAPER DOLLS WITH LACE-ON COSTUMES* - Box (6068)-[Michele & Carolyn]
1026 *TOODLES,* a walking paper doll - Box (4416)
1050 *STORYBOOK PAPER DOLL* (4187)
1051 *MARDI GRAS* (4408)
1052 *WESTERN PAPER DOLLS* (4448)
1053 *SHIRLEY TEMPLE* 1959 (4435)
1054 *FLOWER GIRLS* (4431)
1055 *CAMPUS QUEENS* (4430)
1056 *ROBIN HOOD* (2748)
1057 *LITTLE MISS ALICE* (4410)
1058 *INDIAN PAPER DOLLS* 1961 (4406)
1059 *DAINTY DOLLIES* (2780)
1060 *PERT AND PRETTY* (2620)-[Hat Box]
1061 *45 TOYS I CAN MAKE* - (has one paper doll) 1934.
1061 *BONNIE LASSIE PAPER DOLLS* (2765)-[Petticoat Dolls]
1062 *LITTLE HONEY COLORING BOOK* (with paper doll)
1073 *ROBINSON CRUSOE'S ISLAND HOME* 1934 - stand-ups
1074 *WALKING PAPER DOLL FAMILY* 1934
1171 *MY BOOK OF PAPER DOLLS*
1178 *FAYE EMERSON PAPER DOLLS* (2722)
1180 *PAPER DOLLS TO CUT OUT AND PAINT* 1918
1184 *THE HAPPY FAMILY* [   ]
1211 *GOLDILOCKS AND THE THREE BEARS* 1970 (4211)
1212 *SWEET SUE* (6092)
1213 *NANNY AND THE PROFESSOR* 1970 (4213)
1214 *PLAYMATES* (4214)
1215 *WOODY WOODPECKER'S HOUSE PARTY* (1344)
1216 *TOODLES A WALKING DOLL* (4416)
1217 *SHAMROCK PAPER DOLLS* (4217)
1218 *SUSAN DEY AS LAURIE* 1972 (4218)

1219 *HEATHER, JILL AND ANNE* - Mini Model Paper Dolls 1971 (6059)
1220 *THROUGH THE YEAR WITH THREE PAPER DOLLS* (1346 Pretty As A Rose)
1221 *WEDDING PAPER DOLLS* 1964/71 (4432)
1222 *BALLET STARS* 1964/71 (4431)
1228 *ROCK-A-BYE BABY* - Box makes a cradle (230)
1243 *MOTHER AND DAUGHTER* 1963/70 (6078)
1244 *TEDDY BEAR SET* 1966/70 (1352 Quintuplets)
1245 *BEST FRIENDS* 1963/70 (1339 Bonnets and Bows)
1246 *WEDDING DAY* 1967/70 (4420)
1247 *TERRI AND TONYA* 1966/70 (4469 Jane Fonda)
1248 *TRICIA* 1970 (4248)
1261 *GULLIVER'S TRAVELS* 1939
1270 *GULLIVER'S TRAVELS* 1939 - Box (1261)
1279 *THREE PAPER DOLLS* - Pretty as a Picture (6068 Bunny, Linda and Carol)
1280 *SLEEPY DOLL* 1971 (4280)
1281 *PAPER DOLLS AROUND THE WORLD* 1964/71 (4433)
1282 *PATCHY ANNIE* (6058)
1283 *NANNY AND THE PROFESSOR* 1971/72 (4213)
1284 *NURSERY PAPER DOLLS* 1963/64 (1341 Baby)
1306 *CHAMPION PAPER DOLLS* 1960 (2757)
1307 *PARADE OF PAPER DOLLS* (2760)
1308 *STAR BRIGHT* 1960 (4420 Sheree North)
1309 *STORYLAND PAPER DOLLS* (2798)
1310 *KIDDIE CIRCUS* (4430)
1311 *PRETTY AS A ROSE* (1346)
1311 *LITTLE MODELS* (4431 Bonnets and Bows)
1312 *BUTTERFLY BALLET* (6093)
1312 *PAGEANT PAPER DOLLS* (4438 Brenda Starr)
1313 *PEPE AND THE SENORITAS* 1961 (2712 Carmen)
1313 *KEWPIE KIN* 1967 (4488)
1314 *ONCE UPON A TIME* (4444 Old Woman)
1314 *BABYLAND* 1963/69 (1341 Baby)
1315 *LITTLE WOMEN* (4445)
1316 *COTTON CUTIES* 1960 (6027 & 6079)
1316 *LITTLE WOMEN* 1963 (1345)
1316 *UNITED NATIONS* (4433)
1316 *PAPER DOLLS OF THE BALLET* (4431)
1316 *ONCE UPON A TIME* (4444 Old Woman)
1317 *THE FLYING NUN* 1968/69 (5121)
1317 *STAR TIME* - From four books - #4420 *SHEREE NORTH,* #6093 *BALLET,* #2763 *ICE FESTIVAL* and #2757 *DOUBLE DATE*
1318 *MOTHER GOOSE* (2758)
1319 *SUGAR 'N SPICE* (2780)
1319 *THE FOUR GEMS* (4440 Hootenanny)
1320 *MINI MOPPETS* 1969 (4440)
1320 *HERE COMES THE BRIDE* (4420)
1320 *SHIRLEY TEMPLE* 1959 - 18" doll (5110)
1321 *MINI MODS* 1969 (4441)
1321 *BEAUTY STAR* (2722 Faye Emerson)
1321 *LITTLE MISS ALICE AND HER DOLLY* (4410)
1322 *SUGAR 'N SPICE* 1969 (4442)
1322 *MOTHER GOOSE PAPER DOLLS* (2758)
1323 *DOLLY AND ME* 1969 (4443)
1323 *AT OUR HOUSE* (1330)
1323 *CHARMING PAPER DOLLS* (2753)
1324 *TINA* (6160)
1324 *KIDDIE CIRCUS* (4430)
1324 *TWEEN AGE* (6169)
1325 *LAUGH-IN* 1969 (6045)
1325 *BUTTERFLY BALLET* (6093)
1326 *KING AND QUEEN* - Mardi Gras (4408)
1326 *A DAY WITH DEBBIE* (4446 Evelyn Rudie)
1327 *SURPRISE PACKAGE* (6189)
1328 *MADAMOISELLE PAPER DOLLS* (6128)
1329 *GARDEN PARTY PAPER DOLLS* (2765 Petticoat)
1330 *MOTHER AND DAUGHTER* (resemble Jackie and Caroline) no date, but published in 1962
1330 *THE KEWPIES* (1332)
1331 *DUTCH TREAT* (2717)
1331 *GINA GILLESPIE* 1962
1332 *THE KEWPIES* 1963
1332 *MOTHER AND DAUGHTER* 1963 (6078)
1333 *TEPEE PAPER DOLLS* (4406)
1333 *SUNSHINE GIRL* (6041)
1334 *WINTER CARNIVAL* (2763)
1334 *BLONDIE* 1968 (4434)
1334 *LITTLE WOMEN* (1345)
1335 *BETTY AND HER PLAY PALS*
1335 *JULIA* 1968 (4435)
1335 *ROUND THE CLOCK* 1963 (2764)
1336 *FINIAN'S RAINBOW* 1968 (4436)
1336 *THE WONDERFUL WORLD OF THE BROTHERS GRIMM* 1963
1336 *PRE TEEN* (6169)
1337 *BONNETS AND BOWS* (1339)
1337 *KISSY PAPER DOLL* 1963
1338 *AMERICAN BEAUTIES* 1953 (4308)
1338 *BABY PAPER DOLL* (2783)
1339 *BONNETS AND BOWS* 1963
1339 *PAPER DOLL PLAYMATES* (4451)

1340 *TINY DOLL PARADE* 1963 - assorted dolls from the following books -#4444, #6189, #2780, #2608, #4186, and #2618
1340 *BABY BROTHER* (2783)
1340 *HERE COMES THE BRIDE* 1967 (4420)
1341 *BABY PAPER DOLLS* 1963
1341 *TOODLES THE TODDLER* 1966 (4416)
1342 *WOODY WOODPECKER* (1344)
1342 *BRIDAL PARTY* 1963
1342 *DUTCH TREAT* 1961 (2717)
1343 *DUTCH TREAT* (2717)
1343 *SALLY TWINKLETOES* 1966 (4415)
1344 *WALTER LANTZ CARTOON STARS* 1963 - Woody Woodpecker, Andy Panda, etc.
1344 *KEWPIES IN KEWPIEVILLE* (6088)
1345 *LITTLE WOMEN* 1963
1345 *TINA* (6160)
1346 *KINDERGARTEN* (6020)
1346 *PRETTY AS A ROSE* 1963
1347 *PAPER DOLL PLAYMATES* 1966/1968 (4451)
1347 *GINA GILLESPIE* 1963 (1331)
1348 *MIDI-MOD* 1966 (4439 Judy Doll)
1348 *SHIRLEY TEMPLE* 1959 - 18" doll (5110)
1348 *TRICIA* 1970 (4248)
1349 *TINA* (4449)
1349 *STORYLAND PAPER DOLLS* (2798)
1350 *BABY BROTHER* (2783)
1350 *LITTLE MODELS* (6068 Bunny, Linda and Carol)
1351 *THAT GIRL (MARLO THOMAS)* 1967 (4479)
1351 *JULIET JONES* 1964 (4326)
1352 *SALLY TWINKLETOES* 1966 (4415)
1352 *THE QUINTUPLETS* 1964
1353 *COLONIAL PAPER DOLLS* (1345 Little Women)
1353 *MOTHER AND DAUGHTER* (1330)
1354 *SIX STAND-UP DOLLS FROM STORYLAND* (2798)
1354 *BRIDAL PARTY* (1342)
1355 *PLAYTIME PALS* (6020)
1355 *HEIDI AND PETER* (4187)
1356 *WIGGIE THE MOD MODEL* 1967 (4486)
1356 *CARNIVAL ON ICE* (2763)
1357 *CHARMING PUNCH-OUT PAPER DOLLS* - original from foreign company, new covers drawn
1357 *KAREN* 1965
1358 *WEDDING DAY* 1964/68 (4432)
1358 *COLONIAL PAPER DOLLS* (1345 Little Women)
1358 *MELODY FOUR* (4423 Martha Hyer)
1359 *AROUND THE WORLD PAPER DOLLS, TAKE A TRIP WITH CONNIE AND JEAN* (2767)
1359 *PAPER DOLLS AROUND THE WORLD* 1964 (4433)
1360 *BETSY McCALL* 1965/68 (5120)
1360 *FIESTA* 1965 (2487)
1361 *THE KEWPIES* 1963/67/68 (1332)
1361 *ONCE UPON A TIME* (4444 Old Woman)
1362 *STORYLAND PAPER DOLLS* (4444 Old Woman)
1362 *LILAC TIME* (2779)
1363 *STAR TIME* - from four books - #4420 *SHEREE NORTH*, #6093 *BALLET*, #2763 *ICE FESTIVAL* and #2757 *DOUBLE DATE*
1363 *MOTHER AND DAUGHTER* (6078)
1364 *BALLERINA PAPER DOLLS* (6093)
1365 *10 LITTLE THEATER PAPER DOLLS* (4444 Old Woman)
1366 *PRE TEEN* (6169)
1366 *BONNETS AND BOWS* (1339)
1367 *INDIAN PAPER DOLLS* (4406)
1367 *LET'S PRETEND CIRCUS* (4430)
1368 *DAINTY DOLLY* (4186)
1368 *NURSERY PAPER DOLLS* (1341 Baby)
1369 *FOUR CAMPUS QUEENS* (6128)
1369 *MOD FASHIONS, JANE FONDA* 1966 (4469)
1370 *BETSY McCALL* 1965/66 (5120)
1371 *CAREER GIRLS* (4438 Brenda Starr)
1372 *WOODY WOODPECKER* (1344)
1376 *TINA* (6160)
1377 *LITTLE WOMEN* (1345)
1378 *BUBBLE PARTY* (6092)
1379 *THAT GIRL* 1967 (4479)
1380 *SIX STAND-UP DOLLS FROM STORYLAND* (2798)
1381 *GINGHAM AND CALICO* (6020)
1382 *PAPER DOLL BABIES* (4414 Baby Dears)
1383 *HEIDI AND PETER* (4187)
1384 *CINDERELLA* (2590)
1385 *BALLET PAPER DOLLS* (2616)
1386 *WIGGIE THE MOD MODEL* 1967 (4486)
1387 *THE HAPPIEST MILLIONAIRE* 1967 (4487)
1388 *KEWPIE-KIN* 1967 (4488)
1389 *WEDDING PARTY* (4432)
1390 *BALLET STARS* 1967 (4431)
1391 *WOODY WOODPECKER AND ANDY PANDA* (1344)
1392 *ROOMMATES* (4438 Brenda Starr)
1393 *LITTLE SWEETHEARTS* (1339 Bonnets and Bows)
1394 *BABES IN FAIRYLAND* (1341 Baby)
1406 *CHAMPION PAPER DOLLS* (2757)
1407 *PARADE OF PAPER DOLLS* (2760)
1408 *STAR BRIGHT* (4420 Sheree North)

1409 *STORYLAND* (2798)
1410 *KIDDIE CIRCUS* (4430)
1411 *LITTLE MODELS* 1962 (4431 Bonnets and Bows)
1412 *BUTTERFLY BALLET* (6093)
1413 *PEPE AND THE SENORITAS* 1961 (2712 Carmen)
1414 *ONCE UPON A TIME* (4444 Old Woman)
1415 *LITTLE WOMEN* (4445)
1417 *STAR TIME* - from four books - #4420 *SHEREE NORTH*, #6093 *BALLET*, #2763 *ICE FESTIVAL* and #2757 *DOUBLE DATE*
1418 *MOTHER GOOSE* (2758)
1419 *SUGAR AND SPICE* (2780)
1420 *SHIRLEY TEMPLE* (5110)
1421 *BEAUTY STAR* (2722 Faye Emerson)
1422 *ROMANCE* (2732 Diana Lynn)
1423 *CHARMING PAPER DOLLS* (2753)
1424 *KIDDIE CIRCUS* (4430)
1425 *BUTTERFLY BALLET* (6093)
1426 *KING AND QUEEN* (4408)
1427 *SURPRISE PACKAGE* 1962 (6189)
1428 *MADAMOISELLE PAPER DOLLS* (6128)
1429 *GARDEN PARTY* (2765 Petticoat)
1430 *MOTHER AND DAUGHTER* (1330)
1431 *GINA GILLESPIE* (1331)
1432 *KEWPIE PAPER DOLLS* (1332)
1433 *TEPEE PAPER DOLLS* (4406)
1434 *WINTER CARNIVAL* (2763)
1435 *ROUND THE CLOCK* (2764)
1436 *THE BROTHERS GRIMM* (1336)
1437 *KISSY* (1337)
1438 *AMERICAN BEAUTIES* (4308)
1500 *FAVORITE PAPER DOLLS* 1947 (2486)
1502 *SUPERMAN CUT-OUTS* 1940 catalog - stand-ups
1503 *MOTHER, DAD AND US KIDS* 1949 (2564)
1504 *TOP NOTCH PAPER DOLLS* 1948 (2484 Paper Dolls and Wardrobe Box)
1505 *HOUR OF CHARM* 1943 (2481)
1506 *RAGGEDY ANN AND ANDY* (2497)
1507 *ARTIST MODELS* (2489)
1508 *FESTIVAL* 1944 (2431)
1509 *PAPER DOLL PARTY* (2410)
1510 *BABY SPARKLE PLENTY* 1948 (2500)
1511 *PAPER DOLLY BOOK* (2126)
1512 *JUKE BOX* (2484 Paper Dolls and Wardrobe Box)
1513 *OUTDOOR PAPER DOLLS* 1948 (2518)
1514 *MODERN DOLLS* 1943 (2397)
1515 *PAPER DOLL MODELS* 1942 (2295)
1516 *STYLE SHOP* 1943 (2397)
1517 *JUDY AND JOYCE* 1943 (2424)
1518 *FOUR COUSINS* 1941 (2216)
1519 *HENRY AND HENRIETTA* 1938 (2189)
1520 *SMART PAPER DOLLS* 1940 (2242)
1521 *MODEL PAPER DOLLS* (2242)
1522 *EIGHT STANDING DOLLS* 1948 (2583)
1523 *FOUR PLUS FOUR PAPER DOLLS* 1948 (2583)
1524 *FASHION PAPER DOLLS* 1948 (2424)
1525 *CAROL SUE AND HER FRIENDS* 1948 (2421)
1526 *CINDERELLA* 1950 (2590)
1527 *SCHOOL FRIENDS* 1949 (2313)
1528 *COVER GIRL* 1949 (2492 Mary Martin)
1529 *CARMEN PAPER DOLLS* (Rita Hayworth) 1948 (2712)
1530 *JULIA AND MARIE* 1948 (2426)
1531 *HIGH SCHOOL PAPER DOLLS* 1948 (2425)
1532 *PAPER DOLLS AT PLAY* 1950 (2576)
1533 *MARY AND JO* 1950 (2709 Deluxe)
1534 *FIVE BABY PAPER DOLLS* 1950 (2348)
1535 *HOLLYWOOD FASHIONS* 1949 (2427 Mary Martin)
1536 *JOLLY JUNIORS* 1950 (2713 Pasting Without Paste)
1537 *LOTS OF LITTLE PAPER DOLLS* 1949 (2313)
1538 *HEDY LAMARR* 1951 (2600)
1539 *MARY MARTIN* 1942 (2427)
1540 *ANIMAL PAPER DOLLS TO DRESS* 1950 (2598)
1541 *WESTERN DOLLS* 1950 (2716 Riders of the West)
1542 *GIGI PERREAU* 1951 (2605)
1543 *CHOOSE YOUR PARTNERS* 1951 (2717 Square Dance)
1544 *VANITY PAPER DOLLS* 1951 (2425)
1545 *DORA PAPER DOLLS* 1951 (2604)
1546 *PAPER DOLLS AND THEIR DOLLIES* 1951 (2608 Sweetheart)
1547 *PAPER DOLL CUT-OUTS AND COSTUMES* 1951 (2715 - Pasting Without Paste)
1548 *LOVELY LADY* 1948 (2475)
1549 *DAISY MAE AND LI'L ABNER* 1951 (2360)
1550 *HERE COMES THE BRIDE* 1951 (2882)
1551 *BABS* 1951 (2883)
1552 *PEGGY* 1951 (2884)
1553 *SALLY* 1951 (2885)
1554 *WESTERN PAPER DOLLS* 1950 (2716 Riders of the West)
1555 *HEDY LAMARR* 1951 (2600)
1556 *WEDDING PAPER DOLLS* 1951 (2721)
1557 *FAYE EMERSON* 1952 (2722)
1558 *CARMEN MIRANDA* 1952 (2723)
1559 *BONNY BRAIDS* 1951 (2724)
1562 *CIRCUS PAPER DOLLS* (2610)
1563 *WINTER GIRL WENDY, SUMMER GIRL SUE* 1952 (2611)
1564 *PALS AND PETS* (2612)

1565 *MOTHER AND DAUGHTER* 1952 (2424)
1566 *BIG SISTER AND LITTLE SISTER* 1952 (2424)
1567 *BEST FRIENDS* 1952 (2400)
1568 *MARY AND PAT* 1952 (2400)
1569 *NURSE AND DOCTOR* 1952 (2613)
1570 *PICNIC PAPER DOLLS* 1952 (2614)
1571 *HAPPY BIRTHDAY PAPER DOLLS* 1952 (2615)
1573 *SUMMER DATE* 1948 (2518)
1574 *THE WELL DRESSED GIRL* (2451)
1575 *BALLET PAPER DOLLS* 1953 (2616)
1575 *SOUTHERN BELLES* (2618)
1576 *MERRY TEENS* 1953 (2617)
1577 *CALICO CUT-OUTS* 1953 (2730)
1578 *JOAN CAULFIELD* 1953 (2725)
1579 *DIANA LYNN* 1953 (2732)
1580 *PRETTY PAPER DOLLS* 1953 (4309)
1581 *LARAINE DAY* (2731)
1582 *SOUTHERN BELLES* 1953 (2618)
1583 *BEST FRIENDS* 1953 (2619)
1584 *LINDA DARNELL* 1953 (2733)
1585 *EVE ARDEN* 1953 (4310)
1586 *MARILYN MONROE* 1953 (4308)
1587 *ARLENE DAHL* 1953 (4311)
1588 *BELLE OF THE BALL* 1948 (2492 Mary Martin)
1589 *DOLLS YOU LOVE TO DRESS* 1949 (2438)
1590 *PRETTY AS A PICTURE* 1954 (2426)
1591 *JUDY HOLIDAY* 1954 (2734)
1592 *JUNE AND STU ERWIN* 1954 (2735)
1593 *HAT BOX* (2620)
1594 *PERT AND PRETTY* 1954 (2621)
1595 *LITTLE TODDLERS* 1954 (2736)
1596 *BARBARA BRITTON* 1954 (4318)
1597 *OZZIE AND HARRIET* 1954 (4319)
1598 *MY LITTLE MARGIE* 1954 (Gale Storm) (2737)
1599 *TOWN AND COUNTRY* (2622)
1600 *PAPER DOLL PATSY AND HER PALS* 1954 (2738)
1601 *PRINCE VALIANT AND PRINCESS ALETA* 1954 (4321)
1602 *STYLE SHOW PAPER DOLLS* (2701 Teen Shop)
1603 *PAPER DOLLS WITH GLAMOUR GOWNS* (2739)
1604 *RHONDA FLEMING* (4320)
1605 *GIRL FRIEND - BOY FRIEND* 1955 (2740)
1606 *BEAUTY QUEEN* (2742)
1607 *JULIET JONES* 1955 (4326)
1608 *PAPER DOLL PLAYMATES* 1955 (2743)
1609 *JANE RUSSELL* 1955 (4328)
1610 *CINDERELLA* 1950 (2590)
1611 *WEDDING PARTY* (2721)
1612 *WESTERN PAPER DOLLS* (2716 Riders of the West)
1613 *CHOOSE YOUR PARTNER* (2717 Square Dance)
1614 *LORETTA YOUNG* (4352)
1615 *PAPER DOLLS AND THEIR DOLLIES* (2608 Sweetheart)
1616 *SIX PRETTY PAPER DOLLS* 1956 (2713 and 2715 Pasting Without Paste)
1632 *TIPPY TEEN* - Coloring Book with paper dolls 1967 (4612)
1661 *GLORIA JEAN* 1940
1664 *GLORIA JEAN* 1941
1666 *GLORIA JEAN* 1941
1680 *GLORIA JEAN* 1940 - Box (1661)
1682 *GLORIA JEAN* 1941 - Box (1664)
1683 *GLORIA JEAN* 1941 - Box (1666)
1706 *EVE ARDEN* 1956 (4310)
1707 *BABY SITTER* (2747)
1708 *ROBIN HOOD AND MAID MARIAN* 1956 (2748)
1709 *NURSE AND DOCTOR* (2613)
1710 *SHIRLEY*
1710 *BABY BROTHER* (2783)
1710 *SUMMER GIRL SUE AND WINTER GIRL WENDY* (2611)
1711 *HAPPY BIRTHDAY* (2615)
1711 *MOLLY*
1711 *ROBIN HOOD AND MAID MARIAN* (2748)
1712 *MERRY TEENS* (2617)
1712 *MELISSA*
1712 *WEDDING PARTY* (2721)
1713 *PRETTY PAPER DOLLS* (4309)
1713 *JUDY*
1713 *INDIAN PAPER DOLLS* (4406)
1713 *MOTHER GOOSE* (2758)
1714 *LITTLE TODDLERS* 1958 (2736)
1714 *MOTHER GOOSE* (2758)
1714 *PAPER DOLL MODELS - SUE AND PAM* (2766)
1714 *PLAY CIRCUS* (4430)
1715 *BABY BROTHER* (2783)
1715 *INDIAN PAPER DOLLS* (4406)
1715 *SHIRLEY TEMPLE STANDING DOLLS* 1935
1716 *DAINTY DOLLY* 1962 (4186)
1716 *BALLET PAPER DOLLS* (2616)
1716 *JUDY* (1713)
1717 *MOLLY* (1711)
1717 *POLKA DOT DARLINGS* (6027)
1717 *INDIAN PAPER DOLLS* (4406)
1717 *PLAYTIME PALS* (6020)
1718 *BALLERINA PAPER DOLLS* (6093)
1718 *ANGEL PAPER DOLLS* 1957 (2755)
1718 *SHIRLEY* (1710)

1718 *SOUTHERN BELLES* (2618)
1718 *CINDERELLA* 1950 (2590)
1719 *MELISSA* (1712)
1719 *SHIRLEY TEMPLE STANDING DOLL* 1935 - Box
1719 *SOUTHERN BELLES* (2618)
1719 *CHARMING PAPER DOLLS* 1957 (2753)
1719 *MARDI GRAS* (4408)
1720 *LITTLE MISS ALICE* (4410)
1720 *DATE TIME* (2740)
1720 *A DAY WITH DIANE* (2764)
1720 *KIM NOVAK* 1957 (4409)
1721 *THE WELL DRESSED GIRL IN PAPER DOLLS* (2451)
1721 *PERT AND PRETTY* (2620)
1721 *LITTLE MISS ALICE* 1957 (4410)
1721 *PARTY PLAY* - (4431 for the clothes, dolls [   ]
1722 *IN OLD NEW YORK* 1957 (4411)
1722 *BONNIE LASSIE* (2765)
1723 *FIESTA PAPER DOLLS* (2487)
1723 *DOUBLE DATE* 1957 (2757)
1723 *ROSITA PAPER DOLLS* (2712)-[Carmen-Rita Hayworth]
1724 *PAPER DOLLS FROM MOTHER GOOSE* 1957 (2758)
1724 *BONNY PAPER DOLLS* (6079)-[Darling Doll Box]
1724 *PLAY CIRCUS* (4430)
1725 *STYLE SHOW* (2701)-[Teen Shop]
1725 *SPANKY AND DARLA* 1957 - Little Rascals - (2759)
1725 *SHIRLEY TEMPLE* 1960 (4435)
1726 *LEADING LADIES* (2733)
1726 *SANDRA DEE* (4413)
1726 *MAJORETTE* 1957 (2760)
1727 *SHIRLEY TEMPLE* (4435)
1727 *MY VERY OWN PAPER DOLL DOLLIES* (6189) Only the two small dolls are used
1727 *SHIRLEY TEMPLE STANDING DOLL* - Box 1935
1727 *THE STORY PRINCESS* 1957 - Alene Dalton (2761)
1728 *SHIRLEY TEMPLE DOLLS* - Box - 1939 catalog [   ]
1728 *STORYBOOK PAPER DOLLS* (4187)
1728 *SHEREE NORTH* 1957 (4420)
1728 *RAGGEDY ANN* 1961 - Raggedy Andy is on back cover (2497)
1728 *NANNY AND THE PROFESSOR* 1970 (4213)
1729 *PAPER DOLL CUT-OUTS AND COSTUMES* (2715) -[Pasting Without Paste]
1729 *PATTY AND JEFF* (2736)-[Little Toddlers]
1729 *FLOWER GIRLS* (4431)
1730 *SUGAR 'N SPICE* (4186)
1730 *BEST FRIENDS* (2619)
1730 *CINDERELLA* (2590)
1731 *ICE FESTIVAL* (2763)
1731 *CINDERELLA* (2590)
1731 *ROSITA* (2712 Carmen)
1732 *HEIDI AND PETER* (4187)
1732 *PLAY CIRCUS* (4430)
1732 *A DAY WITH DIANE* (2764)
1733 *MY TWINS*
1733 *CALYPSO PAPER DOLLS* (2723 Carmen Miranda)
1733 *CURTAIN TIME* (2732 Diana Lynn)
1734 *SENORITA PAPER DOLLS* (2712 Carmen)
1734 *SALLY*
1734 *CAMPUS QUEENS* (4430)
1735 *ANNE*
1735 *BALLERINA* (6093)
1735 *PETTICOAT GIRLS* (2765)
1736 *FASHIONS FOR THE MODERN MISS* (2766)
1736 *HELEN*
1736 *BABY BROTHER* (2783)
1737 *SUE AND PAM* (2766)
1737 *AROUND THE WORLD WITH CONNIE AND JEAN* (2767)
1737 *MY VERY OWN PAPER DOLLIES* (6189)
1738 *MERRY TEENS* 1954 (2717 Square Dance)
1738 *SANDRA DEE* (4413)
1738 *INDIAN PAPER DOLLS* (4406)
1739 *CAREER GIRLS* (2731 Laraine Day)
1739 *SHIRLEY TEMPLE* 1959 (4435)
1739 *MOTHER GOOSE* (2758)
1739 *SHIRLEY TEMPLE PLAYHOUSE* 1935 - Box
1740 *BABY TALK* (4414 Baby Dears)
1740 *LOVELY LADY* 1948 (2722 Faye Emerson)
1740 *STORYBOOK PAPER DOLLS* (4187)
1741 *ROMANCE PAPER DOLLS* (2732 Diana Lynn)
1741 *DAINTY DOLLIES* (2780)
1741 *TEEN PARADE* (2701 Teen Shop)
1742 *HOLIDAY PAPER DOLLS* (2737 My Little Margie)
1742 *COLONIAL PAPER DOLLS* (4411 In Old N.Y.)
1742 *WESTERN PAPER DOLLS* (4448)
1743 *LITTLE BALLET DANCERS* (6093)
1743 *MY TWINS* (1733)
1743 *CAMPUS QUEENS* (4430)
1744 *SALLY* (1734)
1744 *PRETTY AS A PICTURE* (2739 Glamour Gowns)
1744 *FLOWER GIRLS* (4431)
1745 *EVELYN RUDIE* 1958 (4425)
1745 *ANNE* (1735)
1746 *LITTLE FRIENDS* (2736 Little Toddlers)
1746 *LITTLE MISS ALICE* (4410)

1747 *BONNIE LASSIE - LYNETTE AND MAUREEN* (2765)
1748 *PLAY CIRCUS* (4430)
1749 *MY VERY OWN PAPER DOLL DOLLIES* (6189) - The two small dolls are used
1750 *HELEN* (1736)
1751 *FLOWER GIRLS* (4431)
1752 *SUGAR AND SPICE* (4186)
1753 *RING AROUND THE ROSY* (1346 Pretty As A Rose)
1754 *DATE TIME* 1965 (2740 Girl Friend, Boy Friend)
1755 *JO AND SUE* 1970 (2764)
1756 *PARTY PLAY PAPER DOLLS* (4431) for the clothes, dolls [   ]
1757 *SCHOOLMATES* (2759)
1758 *PAPER DOLLS FROM MOTHER GOOSE* 1957 (2758)
1760 *BABY BROTHER* (2783)
1761 *ROBIN HOOD AND MAID MARIAN* (2748)
1761 *SHIRLEY TEMPLE - DOLLS AND DRESSES* 1937
1762 *WEDDING PARTY* (2721)
1763 *INDIAN PAPER DOLLS* (4406)
1765 *SHIRLEY TEMPLE* 1936 - 34" tall
1767 *PLAYTIME PALS* (6020)
1768 *CINDERELLA* 1961 (2590)
1769 *NURSE AND DOCTOR PAPER DOLLS* 1952 (2613)
1769 *SOUTHERN BELLES* 1961 (2618)
1770 *A DAY WITH DIANE* (2764)
1770 *SHIRLEY TEMPLE CHRISTMAS BOOK* 1937 (one paper doll from #1739-Playhouse)
1771 *THE WELL DRESSED GIRL* (2451)
1772 *IN OLD NEW YORK COLONIAL PAPER DOLLS* (4411)
1773 *FIESTA* (2487)
1773 *SHIRLEY TEMPLE* (Movie Wardrobe) 1938
1774 *BONNY PAPER DOLLS* (6079 Darling Doll Box)
1775 *STYLE SHOW* (2701 Teen Shop)
1776 *LEADING LADIES* (2733)
1777 *SHIRLEY TEMPLE* (4435)
1778 *STORYBOOK PAPER DOLLS* (4187)
1779 *FLOWER GIRLS* (4431)
1780 *CINDERELLA* (2590)
1780 *SHIRLEY TEMPLE PLAYHOUSE* 1935 (Book form) (1739)
1781 *ROSITA* (2712)-[Carmen]
1782 *SHIRLEY TEMPLE* 1939
1782 *PLAY CIRCUS* (4430)
1783 *MY TWINS* (1733)
1784 *SALLY* (1734)
1785 *ANNE* (1735)
1786 *HELEN* (1736)
1787 *MY VERY OWN PAPER DOLL DOLLIES* (6189)
1787 *SHIRLEY TEMPLE IN MASQUERADE COSTUMES* 1940
1788 *SANDRA DEE* (4413)
1789 *MY VERY OWN PAPER DOLL DOLLIES* (6189)
1789 *SHIRLEY TEMPLE* 1960 (4435)
1790 *STORYBOOK PAPER DOLLS* (4187)
1791 *DAINTY DOLLIES* (2780)
1791 *ROMANCE PAPER DOLLS* (2732)
1792 *WESTERN* (4448)
1792 *HOLIDAY PAPER DOLLS* (2737)-[My Little Margie]
1793 *CAMPUS QUEEN* (4430)
1793 *BALLET* (6093)
1794 *PRETTY AS A PICTURE* (2739)-[Glamour Gowns]
1794 *FLOWER GIRLS* (4431)
1795 *EVELYN RUDIE* 1958 (4425)
1796 *LITTLE FRIENDS* (2622)
H1851 *SCOOBY DOO* 1975 Coloring book/stand-ups
H1852 *HONG KONG PHOOEY* 1975 - Coloring book/stand-ups
H1853 *KORG* 1975 - Coloring book/stand-ups
C1854 *THE NEW ZOO REVUE* 1975 - Coloring book/stand-ups
H1854 *DELVIN* 1975 - coloring book/stand-ups
H1855 *VALLEY OF THE DINOSAURS* 1975 - Coloring book/stand-ups
C1855 *ANIMAL WORLD* 1975 - Coloring book/stand-ups
H1856 *SPEED BUGGY* 1975 - Coloring book/stand-ups
C1861 *RUN JOE RUN* 1975 - Coloring book/stand-ups
1863 *SPACE 1999* - Stand-ups
1902 *FASHION PAPER DOLLS* 1943 (2424)
1916 *STYLE SHOP* 1943 (2397)
1925 *SEVEN PAPER DOLLS* 1939 (885)
1934 *PAPER DOLL DRESS SHOP* 1940 (2193)
1935 *SMART PAPER DOLLS* 1940 - Three books #1, #2, #3 (2242)
1940 *TEN PAPER DOLLS* (2313)
1945 *CLAUDETTE COLBERT* (2503)
1945 *A DOZEN PAPER DOLLS* 1941 (885)
1948 *RITA HAYWORTH* (Carmen) (2712)
1953 *FOUR COUSINS* 1941 (2216)
1954 *BABY DOLLS* 1941
1958 *OUTDOOR PAPER DOLLS* 1941 (2361)
1958 *MY LITTLE MARGIE* 1954 (2737)
1968 *PAPER DOLLY COLORING BOOK* 1942 (2335)
1970 *BIG SISTER PAPER DOLLS* 1942 (2329)
1971 *BROTHER AND SISTER PAPER DOLLS* 1942 (2329)
1972 *TODDLER PAPER DOLLS* 1942 (2329)
1973 *POPULAR PAPER DOLLS* 1943 (2358)
1975 *LET'S PLAY PAPER DOLLS* 1942 - This is Polly, This is Marie (2126)
1976 *PAPER DOLL MODELS* 1942 (2295)
1992 *MY DOLL SUE, MY DOLL LOU* 1942 (2126)
1993 *MY PAPER DOLLS* 1942 (2126)

1993 *PAPER DOLL MODELS* (2295)
1995 *EVELYN RUDIE* 1958 (4425)
2002 *DAISY MAE AND LI'L ABNER* 1943 (2360)
2003 *CAROL SUE AND HER FRIENDS* 1943 (2421)
2004 *MODERN GIRLS* 1943 (2397)
2005 *SKATING STARS* 1943 (2328)
2006 *SIX PRETTY PAPER DOLLS* 1943 (2358)
2051 *THE BOOK OF PAPER DOLL CUT-OUTS* 1927 (includes story) (1180)
2051 *PAPER CUT-OUT DOLLIES* 1927 (includes story) (1180)
2077 *FOUR STANDING DOLLS* (230)
2093 *POPEYE FUNNY FILMS* 1934 - Theater with Popeye Characters
2094 *PAPER DOLL FAMILY AND THEIR HOUSE* 1934
2097 *COMIC PAPER DOLLS* 1935
2099 *MOTHER GOOSE* Stand-ups 1934
2100 *MARY BELLE* 1934 (275)
2106 *PAPER DOLLS AROUND THE WORLD* 1935
2109 *PAPER DOLL FAMILY* 1935
2111 *TOY SOLDIERS* - stand-ups - Box
2112 *SHIRLEY TEMPLE DOLLS AND DRESSES* 1934
2125 *MARIONETTES - A TOY THEATER* 1936 - stand-ups
2126 *POLLY PEPPER PAPER DOLLS* 1936
2128 *PETER RABBIT* - stand-ups 1936
2131 *SCOOTLES AND KEWPIE DOLL BOOK* 1936
2139 *GRANDFATHER'S FARM* 1936 - stand-ups
2140 *HOUSEKEEPING WITH THE KUDDLE KIDDIES* 1936
2141 *GROCERY STORE* to set up 1937 (971)
2142 *THE THREE BEARS* 1937 catalog - stand-ups
2150 *COWBOYS AND INDIANS* 1937 - stand-ups
2158 *SUNNY-DALE FARM* 1937 - stand-ups
2160 *PETUNIA AND PATCHES* 1937
2164 *DRESSES WORN BY THE "FIRST LADIES" OF THE WHITE HOUSE* 1937
2169 *THE TRAILER FAMILY* 1938 - has four stand up dolls but no outfits
2171 *CAPS TO PUT TOGETHER* - Fire Chief, Police Captain, etc.
2172 *TWENTY PAPER DOLLS* 1939 (885)
2173 *DOLLY JEAN* 1938 (877)
2175 *AMERICAN SOLDIERS* 1937 - stand-ups
2176 *LET'S PLAY DOCTOR* 1938
2179 *PAPER DOLLS WITH COSTUMES OF 21 NATIONS* 1938 (2106)
2183 *KITCHEN PLAY* 1938 (with paper dolls)
2185 *BABY DEAR* 1938
2188 *FIRE FIGHTERS IN ACTION* - stand-ups 1938
2189 *HENRY AND HENRIETTA* 1938
2193 *FASHION SHOP* 1938
2194 *LET'S PLAY WEDDING* 1938
2197 *JOLLY PIRATES* 1938 - stand-ups
2205 *TWENTY FOUR CUT OUT BOATS* 1938 - stand-ups
2216 *THE PRINCESS PAPER DOLL BOOK* 1939
2224 *TEN PAPER DOLLS* (230)
2226 *MARY AND SUE* 1939 (275) and (956)
2227 *PAPER DOLLS OF ALL NATIONS* 1939 - Worlds Fair Edition (2106)
C2231 *THE NEW ZOO REVUE* 1974
2232 *PUNCH-OUT DRAG RACING* 1974 - stand-ups
C2232 *PLANET OF THE APES* - stand-ups
2241 *PETER RABBIT STAND-UP STORY BOOK* 1974
2242 *HOLLYWOOD FASHION DOLLS* 1939
2242 *EASTER FUN PUNCH-OUTS* 1974 - stand-ups
2245 *GOLDILOCKS AND THE THREE BEARS* 1939
C2272 *STAR TREK* - Punch-out and Play Book 1975
2280 *THE KEWPIES* - A Coloring and cut-out book 1962 (9553)
2284 *RUTH E. NEWTON'S PAPER DOLL CUT-OUTS* 1940
2295 *PAPER DOLLS ON PARADE* 1940
2296 *PAPER DOLLS* 1940 (230)
2298 *PAPER DOLL PLAYMATES* 1940 catalog (885)
2299 *PAPER DOLLS AROUND THE WORLD* (2106)
2313 *50 PAPER DOLLS* 1940
2321 *TIPTOP PAPER DOLLS* 1940
2328 *SKATING PARTY PAPER DOLLS* 1941
2329 *14 GOOD LITTLE DOLLS* 1941
2335 *CHILDREN OF AMERICA* - Coloring/paper doll book 1941
2348 *THE BADGETT QUADRUPLETS* 1941
2349 *FOUR PLAYMATES* (2126)
2356 *CHARLIE CHAPLIN AND PAULETTE GODDARD* 1941
2358 *LITTLE MISS AMERICA* 1941
2360 *DAISY MAE AND LI'L ABNER* 1941
2361 *DEB'S AND SUB DEBS* 1941
2389 *DAISY MAE AND LI'L ABNER* 1942
2397 *THE MODERN MISS IN PAPER DOLLS* 1942
2400 *SCHOOL GIRL* 1942
2408 *JANE ARDEN* 1942
2410 *PAPER DOLL PARTY* 1944
2411 *PAPER DOLLS* - Anna, Bess, Cherry and Dee 1943 (2358)
2421 *3 PAPER DOLL BOOKS* 1942 (in a partial box)
2424 *MOMMY AND ME* 1943
2425 *THE NEW SHIRLEY TEMPLE* 1942
2426 *JOAN CARROLL* 1942
2427 *MARY MARTIN* 1942
2430 *QUIZ KIDS* 1942
C2431 *LITTLE ORPHAN ANNIE ACTIVITY BOOK* (with Paper Dolls) 1974
2431 *FESTIVAL PAPER DOLLS* 1944
C2432 *NEW ZOO REVUE ACTIVITY BOOK* (has paper doll and clothes to color) 1974
2434 *PLANET OF THE APES* - cut and color book 1974

2436 *LITTLE ORPHAN ANNIE* 1943	2613 *PRINCE AND PRINCESS* (2706)
2438 *ANN SOTHERN* 1943	2613 *STYLE SHOW* (2701 Teen Shop)
2440 *WILD WEST CUT-OUTS* - stand-ups	2614 *PICNIC* 1952
2445 *VICTORY PAPER DOLLS* 1943	2614 *CIRCUS PAPER DOLLS* 1964 (4430)
2446 *ARMY AND NAVY WEDDING PARTY* 1943	2614 *DONNA REED* (4412)
2450 *UNCLE SAM'S LITTLE HELPERS* 1943	2614 *PAPER DOLLS WITH GLAMOUR GOWNS* (2739)
2451 *CLAUDETTE COLBERT* 1943	2615 *HAPPY BIRTHDAY* 1952
2458 *SWEETHEART PAPER DOLLS* 1943	2615 *GIRL FRIEND, BOY FRIEND* (2740)
2460 *BOOTS AND HER BUDDIES* 1943	2615 *RAGGEDY ANN AND ANDY* (2497)
2462 *BETTY FIELD* 1943	2615 *JUNIOR VOGUE* 1963 (6128)
2466 *KELLY SISTERS* 1944 - (1782 Shirley Temple)	2616 *BALLET PAPER DOLLS* 1953
2467 *POLLY AND MOLLY IN FANCY DRESS* 1943 (1787 Shirley Temple)	2616 *PRINCE VALIENT AND PRINCESS ALETA* 1954 (4321)
2468 *STAGE DOOR CANTEEN* 1943	2616 *SCHOOL CHUMS* (2759)
2471 *THE SIX MILLION DOLLAR MAN* - stand-ups	2617 *MERRY TEENS* 1953
2475 *LUCILLE BALL* 1944	2617 *DUTCH TREAT* 1961 (2717)
2478 *NANCY AND HER DOLLS* 1944	2617 *JULIET JONES* (4326)
2481 *HOUR OF CHARM* 1943	2618 *SOUTHERN BELLES* 1953
2483 *JUNIORS PAPER DOLLS* 1945 (2400)	2618 *HAPPY BIRTHDAY* 1961 - outfits from #4431 *BONNETS AND BOWS*, #2616 *BALLET*, #4449 *CINDY* and #2760 *MAJORETTE*. Dolls from [ ]
2484 *PAPER DOLLS AND WARDROBE BOX* 1944	2619 *BEST FRIENDS* 1953
2484 *SPACE 1999* - coloring book with paper doll 1976	2619 *THE QUEEN OF DANCE* (2739 Glamour Gowns)
2485 *ROCK-A-BYE BABY* 1945	2620 *HAT BOX* 1954
2486 *BOB AND BETTY* 1945	2620 *WEE FRIENDS* (2622 Town and Country)
2487 *GOOD NEIGHBOR* 1944	2621 *PERT AND PRETTY* 1954
2488 *CARNIVAL* 1944	2621 *FASHIONS* (2779)
2489 *ARTIST MODELS* 1945	2622 *TOWN AND COUNTRY* 1954
2492 *MARY MARTIN* 1944	2622 *HAPPY HOLIDAY* (2723 Carmen Miranda)
2497 *RAGGEDY ANN AND ANDY* 1944	2623 *STYLE SHOW* 1954 (2701 Teen Shop)
2500 *BABY SPARKLE PLENTY* 1948	2623 *POSY PALS* (6041)
2503 *CLAUDETTE COLBERT* 1945	2624 *HONEYMOON PAPER DOLLS* (2740 Girl Friend-Boy Friend)
2510 *THE WONDERFUL WORLD OF THE BROTHERS GRIMM* 1963 (1336)	2625 *LITTLE BALLERINA* (2616)
2511 *NURSERY PAPER DOLLS* (1341 Baby)	2626 *SQUARE DANCE PARTY* 1961 (2717)
2512 *KINDERGARTEN FASHIONS* (1339 Bonnets and Bows)	2627 *WEDDING DAY* 1961 (2721)
2513 *WOODY WOODPECKER AND HIS FRIENDS* 1968 (1344)	2628 *GIRLS OF THE WEST* 1961 (2716 Riders of the West)
2514 *CIRCUS PAPER DOLLS* 1964 (4430)	2629 *PRE-TEEN PAPER DOLLS* 1961 (6116)
2515 *JUNIOR VOGUE* (6128)	2630 *CHA-CHA-CHA* (2487)
2518 *ROMANCE PAPER DOLLS* 1945	2631 *MUSICAL MAJORETTES* 1962 (2760)
2519 *DAINTY DOLLS FOR TINY TOTS* 1946	2632 *CANDY QUEENS* 1962 (2737 My Little Margie)
2520 *PUSH OUT PAPER DOLLS* 1946	2633 *DESIGNER* 1962 (2730 Calico)
2546 *AIR HOSTESS* 1947	2634 *PENNY AND HER PETS* 1962 (2734)
2550 *SCHOOLMATES* 1947	2635 *SANDY* 1962 (2735)
2550 *CIRCUS COLORING BOOK* with stand-ups	2646 *EVE ARDEN* 1956 (4310)
2564 *FAMILY OF PAPER DOLLS* 1947	2647 *BABY SITTER* (2747)
2573 *UNITED NATIONS PAPER DOLLS* (2106)	2648 *ROBIN HOOD AND MAID MARIAN* 1956 (2748)
2576 *HONEY KITTEN* 1948	2649 *WEDDING PARTY* (2749)
2583 *STAND TOGETHER PAPER DOLLS* 1947	2650 *POLKA DOT DARLINGS* (6027)
2584 *16 PAPER DOLLS* 1948	2651 *JANE RUSSELL* 1955 (4328)
2585 *BIG MOMENT* 1948 (2410)	2652 *BALLET PAPER DOLLS* (2616)
2586 *JUKE BOX* 1948 (2484 Paper Dolls and Wardrobe Box)	2653 *CHARMING PAPER DOLLS* (2753)
2587 *SUMMER DATE* 1948 (2518)	2654 *RAGGEDY ANN AND ANDY* (2497)
2589 *LOVELY LADY* 1948 (2475)	2655 *ANGEL PAPER DOLL* (2755)
2590 *CINDERELLA* 1950	2657 *DOUBLE DATE* (2757)
2591 *FIVE BABY PAPER DOLLS* 1948 (2348)	2658 *PAPER DOLLS FROM MOTHER GOOSE* (2758)
2592 *LOTS OF LITTLE PAPER DOLLS* 1949 (2313)	2659 *LITTLE RASCALS* (2759)
2593 *HOLLYWOOD FASHIONS* 1949 (2427 Mary Martin)	2660 *MAJORETTE PAPER DOLLS* (2760)
2594 *SENIOR PROM* 1949 (2425)	2661 *THE STORY PRINCESS* (2761)
2595 *DOLLS YOU LOVE TO DRESS* 1949 (2438)	2662 *JUNIOR MODELS* (4309)
2596 *THE WELL DRESSED GIRL* 1949 (2451)	2663 *ICE FESTIVAL* (2763)
2597 *VANITY PAPER DOLLS* (2425)	2664 *A DAY WITH DIANE* (2764)
2598 *ANIMAL PAPER DOLLS* 1950	2665 *THE PETTICOAT GIRLS* (2765)
2599 *DOLL HOUSE* (2700)	2666 *BELLE OF THE BALL* 1948 (2492)
2600 *HEDY LAMARR* 1951	2666 *FASHIONS FOR THE MODERN MISS* 1957 (2766)
2601 *MARY MARTIN* 1952 (2427)	2667 *AROUND THE WORLD WITH CONNIE AND JEAN* (2767)
2602 *LITTLE DRESSMAKERS* 1949 (2713)	2668 *JULIET JONES* (4326)
2603 *PRINCE AND PRINCESS* 1949 (2706)	2669 *MERRY TEENS* (2717 Square Dance)
2604 *DORA GROWS UP* 1951	2670 *CAREER GIRLS* (2731 Laraine Day)
2605 *GIGI PERREAU* 1951	2671 *FIESTA* (2487)
2606 *BELLE OF THE BALL* 1948 (2492)	2672 *HAPPY BIRTHDAY* (2615)
2606 *MARY AND JO* (2709 Deluxe Mounted Dolls)	2673 *LOVELY LADY* (2722 Faye Emerson)
2606 *SWEETHEART PAPER DOLLS* (2608)	2674 *HOLIDAY* (2737 My Little Margie)
2607 *THE WELL DRESSED GIRL IN PAPER DOLLS* (2451)	2675 *PRETTY AS A PICTURE* (2739 Glamour Gowns)
2607 *PRETTY AS A PICTURE* (2426)	2676 *ROMANCE* (2732 Diana Lynn)
2607 *BRAND NEW BABY* (2718)	2677 *NURSE AND DOCTOR* (2613)
2608 *SWEETHEART PAPER DOLLS* 1951	2678 *LITTLE BALLET DANCERS* (6093)
2608 *DORA GROWS UP* (2604)	2679 *LILAC TIME* (2779)
2608 *CIRCUS* (2610)	2680 *SUGAR AND SPICE* (2780)
2609 *DAISY MAE AND LI'L ABNER* 1951 (2360)	2681 *BONNY* (6079 Darling Dolls)
2609 *FASHIONS FOR THE MODERN MISS* (2766)	2682 *LEADING LADY* (2733 Linda Darnell)
2609 *SOUTHERN BELLES* (2618)	2683 *BABY BROTHER* (2783)
2610 *CIRCUS* 1952	2684 *ROBIN HOOD* (2748)
2610 *HAT BOX* 1954 (2620)	2685 *BRIDE AND GROOM* (2721)
2610 *BALLET PAPER DOLLS* (2616)	2686 *INDIAN PRINCESS* (4406)
2610 *FAIRYTALE PAPER DOLLS* 1963 (1336) (Brother's Grimm)	2689 *PLAYTIME PALS* (6020)
2611 *DIANA LYNN* 1953 (2732)	2690 *CINDERELLA* (2590)
2611 *WINTER GIRL WENDY, SUMMER GIRL SUE* 1952	2691 *MOTHER AND DAUGHTER* (2618 Southern Belles)
2611 *ICE FESTIVAL* (2763)	2692 *ROUND THE CLOCK* (2764)
2611 *JANE RUSSELL* 1955 (4328)	2693 *LUCKY PAPER DOLLS* (2607 Well Dressed) which originated from (2451)
2611 *NURSERY PAPER DOLLS* (1341 Baby)	2694 *PAPER DOLLS WITH EARLY AMERICAN COSTUMES* (4411)
2612 *PALS AND PETS* 1952	2695 *CHAMPION PAPER DOLLS* (2757)
2612 *NANCY TAKES A TRIP* (2767)	2696 *PARADE OF PAPER DOLLS* (2760)
2612 *KINDERGARTEN FASHIONS* 1964 (1339 Bonnets and Bows)	2697 *STAR BRIGHT* (4420)-[Sheree North]
2613 *NURSE AND DOCTOR* 1952	2698 *STORYLAND* (2798)
2613 *BRAND NEW BABY* (2718)	
2613 *WOODY WOODPECKER AND HIS FRIENDS* (1344)	

2699 *FASHIONS FOR THE MODERN MISS* (2766)
2700 *DOLL HOUSE PAPER DOLLS* 1948
2701 *TEEN SHOP PAPER DOLLS* 1948
2701 *BEAUTY QUEEN* 1955 (2742)
2702 *BELLE OF THE BALL* 1948 (2492)
2702 *PAPER DOLL PLAYMATES* (2743)
2703 *PRETTY AS A PICTURE* 1948 (2426)
2703 *BRAND NEW BABY* (2718)
2704 *FASHION PLATE* 1948 (2462)
2704 *DUDE RANCH* (2716 Riders of the West)
2705 *PASTING WITHOUT PASTE PAPER DOLLS* 1950 (2715)
2705 *CLASSMATES* 1948 (1664)
2706 *PRINCE AND PRINCESS* 1949
2706 *SWEETHEART PAPER DOLLS* (2608)
2707 *BRAND NEW BABY* (2718)
2707 *TEN OF US* (2519)
2708 *CIRCUS* (2610)
2708 *FOUR GREAT BIG PAPER DOLLS* 1949
2709 *DELUXE MOUNTED DOLLS WITH DRESSES* 1949
2709 *FASHIONS FOR THE MODERN MISS* (2766)
2710 *GIRL FRIEND - BOY FRIEND* 1954 (2740)
2710 *BALLET PAPER DOLLS* (2616)
2711 *ICE FESTIVAL* (2763)
2712 *CARMEN PAPER DOLLS* - Rita Hayworth 1948
2712 *NANCY TAKES A TRIP* (2767)
2713 *PRINCE AND PRINCESS* (2706)
2713 *PASTING WITHOUT PASTE LITTLE DRESSMAKERS* 1949
2714 *DONNA REED* 1961 (4412)
2715 *RAGGEDY ANN AND ANDY* 1961 (2497)
2715 *PASTING WITHOUT PASTE PAPER DOLLS FOR LITTLE DRESSMAKERS* 1950
2716 *RIDERS OF THE WEST* 1950
2716 *SCHOOL CHUMS* (2759)
2717 *SQUARE DANCE* 1950
2717 *DUTCH TREAT* 1961
2718 *BRAND NEW BABY PAPER DOLLS* 1951
2718 *HAPPY BIRTHDAY* - Outfits from #4431 *BONNETS AND BOWS*, #2616 *BALLET*, #4449 *CINDY* and #2760 *MAJORETTE*. Dolls from [   ]
2719 *RAGGEDY ANN AND ANDY* 1950 (2497)
2719 *THE QUEEN OF DANCE* (2739 Glamour Gowns)
2720 *WEE FRIENDS* (2622 Town and Country)
2721 *WEDDING PARTY* 1951
2721 *FASHIONS - A PAPER DOLL BOOK* (2779)
2722 *HAPPY HOLIDAY* (2723 Carmen Miranda)
2722 *FAYE EMERSON* 1952
2723 *CARMEN MIRANDA* 1952
2723 *POSY PALS* (6041)
2724 *HONEYMOON PAPER DOLLS* 1961 (2740 Boy Friend-Girl Friend)
2724 *BONNY BRAIDS* 1951
2724 *BABY SITTER* 1956 (2747)
2725 *JOAN CAULFIELD* 1953
2725 *LITTLE BALLERINA* (2616)
2726 *SQUARE DANCE PARTY* (2717)
2727 *WEDDING DAY* (2721)
2728 *GIRLS OF THE WEST* (2716 Riders of the West)
2729 *PRE-TEEN* 1961 (6116)
2730 *CALICO CUT-OUTS* 1953
2730 *CHA-CHA-CHA PAPER DOLLS* (2487)
2731 *LARAINE DAY* 1953
2731 *MUSICAL MAJORETTES* (2760)
2732 *DIANA LYNN* 1953
2732 *CANDY QUEENS* (2737 My Little Margie)
2733 *LINDA DARNELL* 1953
2733 *DESIGNER PAPER DOLLS* (2730 Calico)
2734 *PENNY AND HER PETS*
2734 *JUDY HOLIDAY* 1954
2735 *JUNE AND STU ERWIN* 1954
2735 *SANDY*
2736 *THE OLD WOMAN WHO LIVED IN A SHOE* (4444)
2736 *LITTLE TODDLERS* 1954
2737 *MY LITTLE MARGIE* (Gale Storm) 1954
2737 *SWEETHEART PAPER DOLLS* (6160)
2738 *PAPER DOLL PATSY AND HER PALS* 1954
2738 *NANCY TAKES A TRIP* (2767)
2739 *PAPER DOLLS WITH GLAMOUR GOWNS* 1954
2739 *RAGGEDY ANN AND ANDY* (2497)
2740 *GIRL FRIEND-BOY FRIEND* 1954
2740 *HAPPY BIRTHDAY* - Outfits from #4431 *BONNETS AND BOWS*, #2616 *BALLET*, #4449 *CINDY* and #2760 *MAJORETTE*. Dolls from [   ]
2741 *RAGGEDY ANN AND ANDY* 1944 (2497)
2741 *FASHIONS* (2779)
2742 *POSY PALS* (6041)
2742 *BEAUTY QUEEN*
2743 *DONNA REED* 1961 (4412)
2743 *PAPER DOLL PLAYMATES* 1955
2744 *THE QUEEN OF DANCE* (2739)
2744 *BRAND NEW BABY* (2718)
2745 *HAPPY HOLIDAY* (2723)-[Carmen Miranda]
2745 *DUDE RANCH* (2716)-[Riders of the West]
2746 *EVE ARDEN* 1956 (4310)
2746 *PRINCE AND PRINCESS* (2706)
2747 *BABY SITTER* 1956
2747 *SQUARE DANCE PARTY* (2717)

2748 *ROBIN HOOD AND MAID MARIAN* 1956
2749 *BRIDAL PARTY* 1956
2750 *POLKA DOT DARLINGS* 1957 (6027)
2751 *JANE RUSSELL* 1955 (4328)
2752 *BALLET PAPER DOLLS* (2616)
2753 *CHARMING PAPER DOLLS* 1957
2754 *RAGGEDY ANN AND RAGGEDY ANDY* 1957 (2497)
2755 *ANGEL PAPER DOLLS* 1957
2757 *DOUBLE DATE* 1957
2758 *PAPER DOLLS FROM MOTHER GOOSE* 1957
2759 *LITTLE RASCALS - SPANKY AND DARLA* 1957
2760 *MAJORETTE PAPER DOLLS* 1957
2761 *THE STORY PRINCESS* (Alene Dalton) 1957
2762 *JUNIOR MODELS* (4309)
2763 *ICE FESTIVAL* 1957
2764 *A DAY WITH DIANE* 1957
2765 *THE PETTICOAT GIRLS AND THEIR PARTY DRESSES* 1957
2766 *FASHIONS FOR THE MODERN MISS* 1957
2767 *AROUND THE WORLD WITH CONNIE AND JEAN* 1958
2768 *JULIET JONES* 1955 (4326)
2769 *MERRY TEENS* (2717)-[Square Dance]
2770 *CAREER GIRLS* (2731)-[Laraine Day]
2771 *FIESTA DOLLS* (2487)
2772 *FAYE EMERSON* 1952 (2722)
2772 *HAPPY BIRTHDAY* (2615)
2773 *LOVELY LADY* (2722)-[Faye Emerson]
2774 *HOLIDAY PAPER DOLLS* (2737)-[My Little Margie]
2775 *PRETTY AS A PICTURE* (2739 Glamour Gowns)
2776 *ROMANCE* (2732 Diana Lynn)
2777 *NURSE AND DOCTOR* 1952 (2613)
2778 *LITTLE BALLET DANCERS* (6093)
2779 *LILAC TIME* 1959
2780 *SUGAR AND SPICE* 1959
2781 *BONNY PAPER DOLLS* 1959 (6079)
2782 *LEADING LADIES* (2733 Linda Darnell)
2783 *BABY BROTHER* 1959
2784 *ROBIN HOOD AND MAID MARIAN* (2748)
2785 *BRIDE AND GROOM* 1959 (2721)
2786 *INDIAN PRINCESS* (4406)
2788 *STORYLAND PAPER DOLLS* 1960 (2798)
2789 *PLAYTIME PALS* (6020)
2790 *CINDERELLA* (2590)
2791 *MOTHER AND DAUGHTER* (2618 Southern Belles)
2792 *ROUND THE CLOCK* (2764)
2793 *LUCKY PAPER DOLLS* (2607 Well Dressed) which originated from (2451)
2794 *PAPER DOLLS WITH EARLY AMERICAN COSTUMES* (4411 In Old New York)
2795 *CHAMPION PAPER DOLLS* (2757)
2796 *PARADE OF PAPER DOLLS* 1960 (2760)
2797 *STAR BRIGHT* (4420 Sherre North)
2798 *STORYLAND PAPER DOLLS*
2882 *HERE COMES THE BRIDE* 1949 - Box
2883 *BABS* 1949 - Box
2884 *PEGGY* 1949 - Box
2885 *SALLY* 1949 - Box
3401A *FUNORAMA WITH WOODY WOODPECKER AND HIS FRIENDS* 1976. Has paper doll in color, clothes to be colored (1344)
3403A *PATCHWORK PAPER DOLLS* 1971/72 - Has pages in color and uncolored (6059)
3404A *FAVORITE FAIRY TALES* - stand-ups
3407A *HARVEYLAND SAFETY FIRST* 1972 - Coloring/punch-out toys (5116)
3408A *EARLY AMERICA ACTIVITY ALBUM* (Frontier Village-stand-ups) (5118)
3642A *WEDDING PAPER DOLLS* 1964/71 (4432)
3643A *SIX STAND-UP DOLLS FROM STORYLAND* (2798)
3644A *SUGAR AND SPICE* 1969 (4442)
3731 *THE ADAMS FAMILY ACTIVITY BOOK* (with paper dolls)
3754 *SHIP TO SHORE* - War stand-ups
3816 *PROJECT GO* - Space stand-ups
3927 *MY THREE SONS* 1971 coloring/paper doll book
N3941 *PRE-TEEN PAPER DOLLS* (6169)
N3942 *DAINTY DOLLY PAPER DOLLS* (4186)
N3943 *PAPER DOLL PLAYMATES* 1966/68 (4451)
N3944 *KINDERGARTEN PAPER DOLLS* (6020)
3954 *WEDDING DAY* (9619) coloring/paper doll book
N3961 *SUGAR AND SPICE* 1969 (4442)
N3962 *TOODLES* - The Doll That Walks (4416)
N3963 *RANDY AND CHER* 1966 (4439 Judy Doll)
N3964 *BABYLAND* (1341 Baby)
N3965 *MITZI AND SISSY* (4446)
N3966 *THREE YOUNG GALS* (6169)
4009 *REALLY TRULY DOLLS* - Box - (2358)
N4041 *DINAH-MITE* 1974 - Punch-out figures - stand-ups
P4041 *DADDY'S GIRL* 1974
N4042 *FOR MISS AMERICA* - Henrietta Hippo 1974
P4042 *CARNABY STREET DOLLS* 1973 (4260)
N4043 *COLONIAL AMERICA* 1974
P4043 *TEEN SET* 1973 (4262)
P4044 *THE MODELS* 1973 (4263)
N4061 *COLONIAL AMERICA* 1974 (N4043)
D4111 *FOR MISS AMERICA* - Henrietta Hippo 1974 - Box (N4042)
R4111 *THREE STANDING DOLLS WITH LACE-ON COSTUMES* 1975 - Box (6068 Michelle, Elaine etc.)
R4112 *SHORT STOP SUE AND HER WARDROBE* 1975 - Box

R4113 *FIVE LITTLE BELLES* - Box
4128 *SUSAN DEY* (4218)
R4113 *FIVE LITTLE BELLES* — Box
4128 *SUSAN DEY* (4218)
R4131 *SLEEPY DOLL* - Box - (4280)
4157 *PRETTY PAM* 1948 - Box (2467) which originated from (1787)
4158 *NANCY LOU* 1948 - Box (2467) which originated from (1787)
4170 *ROSE* - Box (6028)
4171 *VIOLET* - Box (6028)
4172 *SUSAN* - Box (6028)
4177 *WENDY* 1953 - Box (2611)
4178 *SUE* 1953 - Box (2611)
4182 *ROSE* 1952 - cloth dresses - Box (6028)
4182 *VIOLET* 1952 - cloth dresses - Box (6028)
4182 *SUSAN* 1952 - cloth dresses - Box (6028)
4186 *MY BONNIE LASSIE* 1957
4187 *HEIDI AND PETER* 1957 - Box
4211 *GOLDILOCKS AND THE THREE BEARS* 1970
4212 *SWEET SUE AND HER DOLLY ELLEN* (6092)
4213 *NANNY AND THE PROFESSOR* 1970
4214 *PLAYMATES* - Original was from foreign company, new covers by Saalfield
4215 *WOODY WOODPECKERS HOUSE PARTY* 1966/68 (1344)
4216 *TOODLES A WALKING DOLL* (4416)
4217 *SHAMROCK PAPER DOLLS* - original was from foreign company, new covers
4218 *SUSAN DEY* 1972
4219 *HEATHER, JILL AND ANNE* 1971 (6059 Patchwork)
4220 *THROUGH THE YEAR WITH 3 PAPER DOLLS* (1346 Pretty as a Rose)
4221 *WEDDING PAPER DOLLS* 1964/71 (4432)
4222 *BALLET STARS* 1964/71 (4431)
4230 *MARY, MARY QUITE CONTRARY* 1972
4231 *AMY JO* 1972
4232 *HOLLY* 1972
4233 *BALLET PAPER DOLLS* 1972
4234 *WE THREE* 1969/73 (4440 Mini Moppets)
4235 *SUNBEAM* 1974
4236 *PRINTS AND POLKA DOTS* 1973
4237 *SUZANNE'S WOW WARDROBE* 1967/73 (4486 Wiggie)
4238 *NANNY AND THE PROFESSOR* 1970 (4213)
4240 *FLOWER GIRL* 1966/69 (4452 Sugar Plum)
4241 *TERRI AND TONYA* 1966/70 (4469 Jane Fonda)
4242 *THE TEDDY BEAR SET* (1352 Quintuplets)
4243 *MOTHER AND DAUGHTER* 1963/70 (6078)
4244 *THE TEDDY BEAR SET* 1966/70 (1352 Quintuplets)
4245 *BEST FRIENDS* 1963/70 (1339 Bonnets and Bows)
4246 *WEDDING DAY* 1967/70 (4420)
4247 *TERRI AND TONYA* 1966/70 (4469 Jane Fonda)
4248 *TRICIA* 1970
4249 *SLEEPY DOLL* 1971 (4280)
4250 *TINA* - teenager with change about wigs (6160)
4251 *TOODLES THE TODDLER* 1966 (4416)
4252 *WOODY WOODPECKER AND ANDY PANDA* (1344)
4253 *SIX STAND-UP DOLLS FROM STORYLAND* (2798)
4254 *DOLLY AND ME* 1969 (4443)
4260 *TEEN BOUTIQUE* 1973
4261 *SUSAN DEY* 1972/73 (4218)
4262 *FAVE TEENS* 1973
4263 *GIRLFRIENDS* 1973
4279 *3 PAPER DOLLS "PRETTY AS A PICTURE"* (6068 Bunny, Linda and Carol)
4280 *SLEEPY DOLL* 1971
4281 *PAPER DOLLS AROUND THE WORLD* 1964/71 (4433)
4282 *PATCHY ANNIE* (6058)
4283 *NANNY AND THE PROFESSOR* 1970/71 (4213)
4284 *NURSERY PAPER DOLLS* 1963/64 (1341 Baby)
4286 *A DAY WITH DEBBIE* (4446)
4300 *OLD WEST STAND-UPS* 1952
4304 *TOM CORBETT SPACE CADET PUSH-OUTS* 1952 stand-ups
4305 *CIRCUS PUSH-OUTS* 1953 stand-ups
4308 *MARILYN MONROE* 1953
4309 *BONNIE BOWS* 1953
4310 *EVE ARDEN* 1953
4311 *ARLENE DAHL* 1953
4312 *CORONATION PAPER DOLLS AND COLORING BOOK* 1953
4317 *MEADOW BROOK FARM* - A Punch-out Panorama Book
4318 *BARBARA BRITTON* 1954
4319 *OZZIE AND HARRIET* 1954
4320 *RHONDA FLEMING* 1954 Paper doll/coloring book
4321 *PRINCE VALIANT AND PRINCESS ALETA* 1954
4322 *PLAY TRAIN* 1954 - stand-ups and coloring book
4323 *MARILYN MONROE* 1954 (4308)
4326 *JULIET JONES* 1955 Paper doll/coloring book
4327 *PAPER DOLL PARADE* (12 dolls from 3 books - *SOUTHERN BELLES* #2618, *DORA* #2604 and *SQUARE DANCE* #2717)
4328 *JANE RUSSELL* 1955 Paper Dolls/coloring book
4329 *FINIAN'S RAINBOW* 1968 (4436)
4329 *17 PAPER DOLLS* (from three books #2608 *SWEETHEART*, #2616 *BALLET*, and #2615 *HAPPY BIRTHDAY*)
4330 *FOUR GREAT BIG PAPER DOLLS* (2708)
4343 *CURIOSITY SHOP* 1971
4344 *THE TEDDY BEAR SET* 1966/70 (1352 Quintuplets)
4351 *BEAUTIFUL MODELS* (from 2 books - #2739 *GLAMOUR GOWNS* and #2712 *CARMEN*)

4352 *LORETTA YOUNG* 1956 Paper Doll/Coloring book
4356 *FESS PARKER* 1964 - Stand-ups
4406 *INDIAN PAPER DOLLS AND COLORING BOOK* 1956
4406 *JULIE ANDREWS* (4424)
4407 *CIRCUS PAPER DOLLS* (2610)
4407 *ANN SOTHERN* 1956
4407 *BUTTERFLY BALLET* (6093)
4408 *SUNSHINE GIRL* (6041)
4408 *PEPE AND THE SENORITAS* 1961 (2712) Pepe doll added
4408 *MARDI GRAS* - King and Queen statuette dolls 1956
4409 *RAGGEDY ANN AND ANDY PAPER DOLLS/COLORING BOOK* 1944 (2497)
4409 *KIM NOVAK* 1957 Paper Doll/Coloring Book
4409 *MOTHER GOOSE* (2758)
4410 *LITTLE WOMEN* 1963 (1345)
4410 *LITTLE MISS ALICE PAPER DOLLS AND COLORING BOOKS* 1957
4410 *MARTHA HYER* 1958 (4423)
4410 *DONNA REED* (4412)
4411 *PRETTY AS A ROSE* (1346)
4411 *IN OLD NEW YORK* - Colonial Paper Doll/Coloring Book 1957
4411 *HATBOX* (6068 Janie, Sue and Nancy)
4411 *SIX STAND-UP DOLLS FROM STORYBOOK LAND* (2798)
4412 *DONNA REED* 1959
4412 *PAGEANT PAPER DOLLS* (4438 Brenda Starr)
4412 *GINGHAM AND CALICO CUT-OUTS* (6020)
4413 *SANDRA DEE* 1959
4413 *KEWPIE KIN* 1967 (4488)
4413 *TINA* 1969 (4449)
4414 *BABYLAND* 1963/69 (1341 Baby)
4414 *BABY DEARS* 1959
4415 *ANN SOTHERN* 1959 (4407)
4415 *SALLY TWINKLETOES AND PEGGY TWIRL* 1966
4416 *PAPER DOLLS OF THE BALLET* 1964/69 (4431)
4416 *TOODLES THE TODDLER* - A Walking Paper Doll 1966
4416 *DONNA REED* 1959 (4412)
4417 *SANDRA DEE* 1959 (4413)
4417 *MOD PAPER DOLLS* 1966 (4439 Judy Doll)
4417 *THE FLYING NUN* 1969 (5121)
4418 *HAPPINESS IS BABYLAND* 1966 (1352 Quintuplets)
4418 *BABY DEARS* (4414)
4419 *THE FOUR GEMS* (4440 Hootenanny)
4419 *TUESDAY WELD* 1961 (4432)
4419 *POLLY BERGEN* 1959 (4434)
4419 *ANN SOTHERN* (4407)
4420 *SHIRLEY TEMPLE* 1959 - 18" doll (5110)
4420 *SHEREE NORTH* 1957
4420 *HERE COMES THE BRIDE* 1967
4420 *6 STAND-UP DOLLS FROM STORYBOOKLAND* (2798)
4421 *LITTLE MISS ALICE AND HER DOLLY* (4410)
4421 *BRIDAL PARTY* (2749)
4421 *GISELLE MACKENZIE* 1957
4421 *GINGHAM AND CALICO CUT-OUTS* (6020)
4422 *PAPER DOLL BABIES* (4414 Baby Dears)
4422 *MOTHER GOOSE PAPER DOLLS* (2758)
4422 *DUDE RANCH* (2716 Riders of the West)
4422 *VIRGINIA MAYO* 1957
4423 *AT OUR HOUSE* (1330)-[Mother and Daughter]
4423 *MARTHA HYER* 1958
4423 *MARILYN MONROE* (4308)
4423 *MARDI GRAS* (4408)
4424 *HEIDI AND PETER* 1961 (4187)
4424 *TWEEN-AGE* 1966 (6169)
4424 *JULIE ANDREWS* 1958
4425 *HEIDI AND PETER* (4187)
4425 *GISELE MACKENZIE* 1958 (4428)
4425 *EVELYN RUDIE* 1958
4426 *WEDDING PAPER DOLLS* (4420)
4426 *DOUBLE DATE* 1963 (2757)
4426 *DAINTY DOLLY* 1958 (4186)
4427 *HEIDI AND PETER* 1958 (4187)
4427 *CINDERELLA* (2590)
4428 *GISELLE MACKENZIE* 1958
4428 *BALLET* (2616)
4429 *KIM NOVAK* 1958
4430 *CAMPUS SWEETHEARTS* 1957 (A Carry Doll Kit)
4430 *KIDDIE CIRCUS*
4431 *BALLET PAPER DOLLS* 1964 (Double Doll Book)
4431 *FLOWER GIRLS* (A Carry Doll Kit) 1957
4431 *BONNETS AND BOWS*
4432 *TUESDAY WELD* 1960
4432 *MARTHA HYER* 1958 (4423)
4432 *DOUBLE WEDDING* 1964 - (Double Doll Book)
4433 *UNITED NATIONS* 1964 - (Double Doll Book)
4433 *TAMMY MARIHUGH* 1960
4434 *POLLY BERGEN* 1958
4434 *TUESDAY WELD* 1960/61 (4432)
4434 *BLONDIE* 1968
4435 *SHIRLEY TEMPLE* 1958
4435 *SANDRA DEE* (4413)
4435 *JULIA* 1968
4436 *JOANNE WOODWARD* 1958 (4441)
4436 *FINIAN'S RAINBOW* 1968
4436 *DONNA REED* 1959/64 (4412)
4437 *SHIRLEY TEMPLE* (4435)

4437 *BONNETS AND BOWS* (1339)
4437 *TINA* (4449)
4438 *THREE BABY DOLLS* (4414)-[Baby Dears]
4438 *BRENDA STARR* 1964
4438 *BABY PAPER DOLL* (2783)
4439 *JUDY DOLL* - Miss Teen Age America 1964
4439 *LITTLE CHARMERS* 1960 (4186)
4439 *PAPER DOLL PLAYMATES* 1966/68 (4451)
4440 *SHIRLEY TEMPLE* 1959 (4435)
4440 *HOOTENANNY* 1964
4440 *MINI MOPPETS* 1969
4441 *JOANNE WOODWARD* 1958
4441 *KEWPIES IN KEWPIEVILLE* 1966 (6088)
4441 *MINI MODS* 1969
4441 *SIX STAND-UP DOLLS FROM STORYLAND* (2798)
4442 *SUGAR AND SPICE* 1969
4442 *POLLY BERGEN* 1958 (4434)
4442 *FASHION LAND* (4407)-[Ann Sothern]
4443 *DAINTY DOLLY* (4186)
4443 *DOLLY AND ME* 1969
4443 *A DAY WITH DEBBIE* (4446)
4443 *JEANNIE STAND-UP AND HER KITTY* (4449)
4444 *THE OLD WOMAN WHO LIVED IN A SHOE* 1960
4444 *BALLET* 1966 (2616)
4445 *LITTLE WOMEN* 1960
4446 *EVELYN RUDIE* 1958
4447 *SHARI LEWIS* 1958
4448 *TEXAS ROSE*
4449 *THROUGH THE YEAR WITH CINDY* 1959
4450 *CORONATION PAPER DOLLS AND COLORING BOOK* 1953 (4312)
4451 *PAPER DOLL PLAYMATES* 1966
4451 *JANE RUSSELL* 1955 (4328)
4452 *TOODLES* 1970 (4416)
4452 *SUGAR PLUM PALS* 1966
4452 *17 PAPER DOLLS* - Comes from three books - *BALLET* #2616, *SWEETHEART* #2608, and *HAPPY BIRTHDAY* #2615
4453 *FLOWER GIRLS* (1346)-[Pretty as a Rose]
4453 *FOUR GREAT BIG PAPER DOLLS* (2708)
4454 *BRIGHT EYES* 1966 (6068)-[Carol, Bunny, and Linda]
4454 *BEAUTIFUL MODELS* - From two books - (#2712-*CARMEN* and #2739-*GLAMOUR GOWNS*)
4455 *LORETTA YOUNG* 1956 Paper Doll and Coloring Book (4352)
4456 *JULIE ANDREWS* (4424)
4456 *INDIAN PAPER DOLLS* with pictures to color 1966 (4406)
4457 *CIRCUS PAPER DOLLS* (2610)
4457 *ANN SOTHERN* 1956 (4407)
4457 *BUTTERFLY BALLET* (6093)
4458 *SUNSHINE GIRL* (6041)
4458 *PEPE* (2712 Carmen)
4458 *WEDDING DAY PAPER DOLLS* 1964/68 (4432)
4458 *MARDI GRAS* (4408)
4459 *PAPER DOLLS AROUND THE WORLD* 1964 (4433)
4459 *KIM NOVAK* 1957 Paper Dolls and Coloring Book (4409)
4459 *MOTHER GOOSE* (2758)
4460 *BETSY McCALL* 1965/68 (5120)
4460 *MARTHA HYER* 1958 (4423)
4460 *LITTLE MISS ALICE PAPER DOLLS* 1957 (4410)
4461 *HAT BOX* (6068 Janie, Sue and Nancy)
4461 *KEWPIES WITH KEWPIEVILLE* stand-ups 1968 (1332)
4461 *IN OLD NEW YORK PAPER DOLLS AND COLORING BOOK* 1957 (4411)
4462 *STORYLAND* (4444 Old Woman)
4463 *MOTHER AND DAUGHTER* 1963/68 (6078)
4463 *CIRCUS PAPER DOLLS* with pictures to color (2610)
4464 *PRINCE AND PRINCESS PAPER DOLLS AND COLORING BOOK* 1949 (2706)
4465 *RAGGEDY ANN AND ANDY PAPER DOLLS AND COLORING BOOK* 1944 (2497)
4466 *LET'S PLAY PAPER DOLLS AND COLOR THE PICTURES* (2612 Pals and Pets)
4466 *DONNA REED* 1959 (4412)
4466 *BONNETS AND BOWS* (1339)
4467 *LET'S PLAY PRETEND CIRCUS PAPER DOLLS* (4430)
4467 *SANDRA DEE* 1959 (4413)
4467 *PAPER DOLL PATSY AND HER PALS* (from two books - #2738 *PAPER DOLL PATSY* and #2619 *BEST FRIENDS*)
4468 *12 PAPER DOLLS AT PLAY* (from two books - #2743 *PLAYMATES* & #2614 *PICNIC*)
4468 *NURSERY PAPER DOLLS AND PUNCH-OUTS* 1963/64 (1341 Baby)
4468 *BABY DEARS* 1959 (4414)
4469 *JANE FONDA - MOD FASHIONS* 1966
4469 *ANN SOTHERN* 1956 (4407)
4469 *LITTLE FRIENDS* - a double book (2622 Town and Country)
4470 *BETSY McCALL* 1965/66 (5120)
4470 *SHIRLEY TEMPLE* 1959 - 18" Doll (5110)
4470 *SHEREE NORTH* (4420)
4471 *BRIDAL PARTY* (2749)
4471 *CAREER GIRLS* (4438 Brenda Starr)
4471 *MARLO THOMAS AS "THAT GIRL"* 1969 (4479)
4471 *GISELE MACKENZIE* (4421)
4472 *JULIA* 1968/69 (4435)
4472 *DUDE RANCH* (2716 Riders of the West)
4472 *VIRGINIA MAYO* 1957 (4422)

4472 *COSTUME PARTY WITH WOODY WOODPECKER AND FRIENDS* 1966 (1344)
4473 *MARTHA HYER* (4423)
4473 *MARDI GRAS* (4408)
4473 *FLOWER GIRL PAPER DOLLS* 1966/69 (4452 Sugar Plum)
4474 *PETITE PAPER DOLLS* (6068 Bunny, Linda and Carol)
4474 *JULIE ANDREWS* 1958 (4424)
4474 *HEIDI AND PETER* (4187)
4475 *WHITE HOUSE* 1969
4475 *GISELLE MACKENZIE* 1958 (4428)
4475 *EVELYN RUDIE* 1958 (4425)
4475 *BABY BROTHER* 1959 (2783)
4476 *DAINTY DOLLY* 1958 (4186) .
4476 *TINA* (6160)
4476 *KINDERGARTEN* 1969 (6020)
4477 *HEIDI AND PETER* (4187)
4477 *LITTLE WOMEN* (1345)
4478 *GISELLE MACKENZIE* 1958 (4428)
4478 *BUBBLE PARTY* (6092)
4479 *KIM NOVAK* 1958 (4429)
4479 *MARLO THOMAS AS "THAT GIRL"* 1967
4479 *THROUGH THE YEAR WITH CINDY* (4449)
4480 *CAMPUS SWEETHEARTS* - A Carry Doll Kit (4430)
4480 *KIDDIE CIRCUS* (4430)
4481 *BONNETS AND BOWS* (4431)
4481 *FLOWER GIRLS* (4431)
4484 *POLLY BERGEN* 1958 (4434)
4485 *SHIRLEY TEMPLE* (4435)
4486 *WIGGIE, THE MOD MODEL* 1967
4486 *JOANNE WOODWARD* 1958 (4441)
4487 *HAPPIEST MILLIONAIRE* 1967
4487 *SHIRLEY TEMPLE* (4435)
4488 *KEWPIE KIN* 1967
4488 *3 BABY DOLLS* (4414 Baby Dears)
4489 *WEDDING PARTY* 1964/1967 (4432)
4489 *LITTLE CHARMERS* 1960 (4186)
4490 *SHIRLEY TEMPLE* (4435)
4490 *BALLET STARS* 1967 (4431)
4491 *JOANNE WOODWARD* (4441)
4491 *FLOWER GIRLS* 1957 - A Carry Doll Kit (4431)
4491 *WOODY WOODPECKER AND ANDY PANDA* 1966/1968 (1344)
4492 *ROOMMATES* (4438 Brenda Starr)
4492 *POLLY BERGEN* 1958 (4434)
4493 *LITTLE SWEETHEARTS* 1963/1968 (1339 Bonnets and Bows)
4493 *JEANNIE* - A Stand-up Paper Doll and Her Kitty (4449)
4493 *DAINTY DOLLY* (4186)
4494 *BABES IN FAIRYLAND* 1963/1968 (1341 Baby)
4494 *THE OLD WOMAN WHO LIVED IN A SHOE* (4444)
4495 *TRICIA* 1970 (4248)
4495 *LITTLE WOMEN* 1960 (4445)
4512 *TIPPY TEEN* 1967 - Paper Doll/Coloring Book (4612)
4513 *SHIRLEY TEMPLE BUSY BOOK* 1959 - Paper doll of Shirley's doll (5326)
4515 *STORY OF THE BALLET* 1964 - Paper Doll/Coloring Book (9568)
4517 *BALLET COLORING BOOK* 1963/1964 Paper Doll/Coloring book (9568)
4580 *ONCE UPON A WEDDING DAY* - Paper Doll/Coloring book (9619)
4586 *ONCE UPON A WEDDING DAY* - Paper Doll/Coloring book (9619)
4615 *BALLET COLORING BOOK* 1963/64 (9568)
4612 *TIPPY TEEN* 1967 - Coloring book/paper dolls
4695 *THE ADDAMS FAMILY* 1965 - Coloring book/stand-ups
5017 *MODERN GIRLS* 1950 (2216)
5033 *PAPER DOLLS TO DRESS* 1951 - Box with 4 books from #2882, #2883, #2884, and #2885.
5110 *SHIRLEY TEMPLE* 1958
5111 *CANDY STRIPERS* 1973
5111 *SANDRA DEE* 1959 - Box (4413)
5112 *LOST HORIZON* 1973
5112 *TUESDAY WELD* 1960 - Box (4432)
5113 *CLASSIC BOUTIQUE* (originated from two foreign books)
5114 *NANNY AND THE PROFESSOR* 1970/1971 (4213)
5115 *DODIE* from "My Three Sons" 1971
5116 *HARVEYLAND SAFETY FIRST* 1972 - Play book
5118 *EARLY AMERICAN ACTIVITY ALBUM* - Frontier Village - stand-ups
5119 *FUNORAMA* - Woody Woodpecker and Andy Panda 1972 (1344)
5120 *BETSY McCALL* 1965
5121 *THE FLYING NUN* 1968
5122 *MODELS OF TODAY* (4439 Judy Doll)
5123 *THE HAPPY BRIDE* (6054)
5124 *THE FLYING NUN* 1968/1969 (5121)
5125 *BOUTIQUE PAPER DOLLS* 1968 (4439 Judy Doll)
5126 *MOTHER GOOSE PAPER DOLLS* (2758)
5127 *LITTLE WOMEN* (1345)
5128 *WEDDING DAY* (6054)
5129 *LITTLE GIRLS ARE EVERYTHING NICE* (5229)
5130 *BETSY McCALL* 1965 (5120)
5131 *THE FLYING NUN* 1968 (5121)
5132 *MODELS OF TODAY* (4439 Judy Doll)
5133 *HAPPY BRIDE* (6054)
5134 *THE FLYING NUN* 1968 (5121)
5135 *BOUTIQUE PAPER DOLLS* 1968 (4439 Judy Doll)
5136 *MOTHER GOOSE* (2758)
5137 *THE PARTRIDGE FAMILY* 1971
5138 *PATCHWORK PAPER DOLLS* 1971 (6059)
5139 *HEE HAW* 1971

5140 *JULIA* 1968/1971 (4435)
5141 *THE PARTRIDGE FAMILY* 1971 (5137)
5141 *DARLING PAPER DOLLS* 1969 (4452 Sugar Plum)
5142 *CIRCUS STARS* (4430)
5143 *THE PARTRIDGE FAMILY* 1971/1972 (5137)
5145 *PATCHWORK PAPER DOLLS* 1971/1972 (6059)
5151 *SIX STANDING DOLLS* 1942 - Box (Copyrighted before the original #2410)
5153 *TONY* 1949 - Box (2425)
5154 *MARCELLA* 1949 - Box (2425)
5160 *BABY SPARKLE PLENTY* 1948 (pictured with #2500)
5160 *SHIRLEY TEMPLE* 1958 (5110)
5161 *DEBBIE DARLING* - Box (6027)
5161 *CARMEN PAPER DOLLS* - Rita Hayworth 1948 - Box (2712)
5162 *BETTY DARLING* (6027)
5163 *HARMONY STREET ACTIVITY BOOK* 1971
5163 *RANCHLAND* 1952 - Box (2716 Riders of the West)
5164 *PETS TO DRESS* 1952 - Box (2598)
5165 *FASHION FUN* 1952 - Box (2715 Pasting Without Paste)
5166 *BRIDE AND GROOM* 1952 - Box (2721)
5167 *BONNY BRAIDS* 1951 - Box (2724)
5169 *DEBBIE DARLING* 1952 - Box (6027)
5170 *DIANE DARLING* - Box (6079)
5171 *THE PARTRIDGE FAMILY* - Pictorial Activity Album 1973 includes stand-ups
5171 *DOTTIE DARLING* - Box (6079)
5172 *DEBBIE DARLING* - Box (6027)
5173 *BETTY DARLING* - Box (6027)
5176 *NURSE AND DOCTOR* - Box (2613)
5177 *BIRTHDAY PARTY* - Box 1953 (2615)
5178 *PAPER DOLLS FROM 6 TO 16* - Box (2604)
5180 *JEANNETTE* - Box 1954
5181 *CORINNE* - Box 1954
5183 *DIANA LYNN* - Box 1953 (2732)
5184 *LINDA DARNELL* - Box 1953 (2733)
5187 *DIANE DARLING* 1957 - Box (6079)
5188 *DOTTIE DARLING* 1957 - Box (6079)
5190 *BARBARA BRITTON* 1954 - Box (4318)
5191 *RHONDA FLEMING* 1954 - Box (4320)
5194 *COLONIAL PAPER DOLLS* with Magic Stay-On Costumes - Box (4411)
5195 *LITTLE MISS ALICE* - Box (4410)
5196 *EVELYN RUDIE* 1958 - Box (4425)
5197 *DONNA REED* 1960 - Box (4412)
5214 *CRADLE BABY* 1948
5215 *PAPOOSIE* 1949 - Has doll and story, no outfits
5219 *RIDE EM COWBOY* - stand-ups
5219 *FUNORAMA WITH WOODY WOODPECKER AND HIS FRIENDS* 1964 (1344)
5221 *SANTA CLAUS PUSH-OUTS* (ornaments for tree)
5224 *THE MANGER SCENE* - stand-ups
5225 *MARIE OSMOND* 1973
5229 *LITTLE GIRLS ARE EVERYTHING NICE* - originated from a foreign set of paper dolls with new covers drawn
5230 *MARY, MARY QUITE CONTRARY* 1972 (4230)
5231 *AMY JO* 1972 (4231)
5232 *HOLLY* 1972 (4232)
5233 *BALLET PAPER DOLLS* 1972 (4233)
5234 *WEE THREE* 1969/1973 (4440 Mini Moppets)
5235 *SUNBEAM* 1974 (4235)
5236 *PRINTS AND POLKA DOTS* 1973 (4236)
5237 *SUZANNE'S WOW WARDROBE* 1967/1973 (4486 Wiggie)
5242 *CIRCUS STARS*, 7 Little Performers (4430)
5243 *THE PARTRIDGE FAMILY* 1974 (5137)
5246 *SUMMERTIME SUE, WINTERTIME WENDY* 1974
5261 *FAVORITE FAMILY* - stand-ups
5291 *SANTA'S PUNCH-OUTS* - stand-ups
5292 *MERRY CHRISTMAS BUSY BOOK* - things to make, etc. no paper dolls
5326 *SHIRLEY TEMPLE BUSY BOOK* - paper doll of Shirley's doll
5526 *SHIRLEY TEMPLE BUSY BOOK* (5326)
6005 *PERSONALITY PAPER DOLLS* (2400)
6020 *PRESCHOOL PAPER DOLLS* 1958 - Box
6021 *KISSY - A PAPER DOLL* 1965 - Box (1337)
6024 *THE HAPPY BRIDE* - Box (2749)
6024 *SUSAN DEY* 1972 - Box (4218)
6025 *SUE, A "JUST LIKE ME" DOLL* 1958 - Box (6117)
6027 *DARLING DOLLS WITH WAVY HAIR* 1952 - Box
6027 *SLEEPY DOLL* 1971/1973 (4280)
6028 *LOVELY DOLLS WITH REAL CLOTH DRESSES* 1952 - Box
6029 *DARLING DOLLS WITH WAVY HAIR* 1961 - Box (6194)
6030 *SHIRLEY TEMPLE PLAY KIT* 1958 (9859)
6032 *SHIRLEY TEMPLE PLAY KIT* 1958 (9859)
6033 *DARLING DOLLS* - Box (6027)
6039 *DARLING DOLLS WITH WAVY HAIR* - Box (6194)
6040 *KATHY, A "Just Like Me" Doll* - Box (6117)
6040 *PRESCHOOL PAPER DOLLS* - Box (6020)
6041 *MARY LOU - A DARLING DOLL WITH WAVY HAIR* 1958 - Box
6042 *LITTLE AUDREY'S DRESS DESIGNER KIT* 1962
6043 *SHARI LEWIS AND HER PUPPETS* 1963 - Box (6060)
6044 *LOVELY DOLLS WITH REAL CLOTH DRESSES* - Box (6028)
6044 *DODIE* 1971 - Box (5115)
6045 *LAUGH-IN PARTY* 1969 - Box
6048 *CANDY STRIPERS* 1973 - Box (5111)
6049 *CURIOSITY SHOP ACTIVITY* (finger puppets) - Box

6050 *THE PARTRIDGE FAMILY* - Box (5137)
6052 *SWEETHEART DOLLS* 1954 - Box
6053 *BLONDIE* 1968 - Box (4434)
6054 *HAPPINESS IS LEARNING HOW* (with weatherman paper doll) 1973 -Box
6054 *ELIZABETH THE BEAUTIFUL BRIDE* 1966
6055 *DAISY A DARLING DOLL WITH WAVY HAIR* - Box (6169)
6055 *JULIA* 1968 (4435)
6055 *JULIA* 1970 - Box (4435) Inside pages are dated 1968
6056 *LITTLE AUDREY'S DRESS-UP PLAY DOLL* - A standing doll (6042)
6056 *DOLLY AND ME* 1969 - Box (4443)
6057 *FASHION WHIRL PAPER DOLLS* 1968/1970 - Boxed Game
6058 *THE HOLIDAY TWINS* - Betty and Bobby 1970 - Box
6058 *PATCHY ANNIE "THE ROCKAWAY DOLL"* 1962 - Box
6059 *HERE COMES THE BRIDE* - Box (2749) Date is 1956
6059 *PATCHWORK* 1971 - Box
6060 *SHARI LEWIS AND HER PUPPETS* 1960 - Box
6060 *SUGAR AND SPICE* 1971 (4442)
6061 *MAKE BELIEVE AND PLAY STEWARDESS* 1970 - Box
6062 *MARLO THOMAS AS "THAT GIRL"* 1969 - Box (4479)
6063 *PRE-SCHOOL PAPER DOLLS* - Box (6020)
6064 *KINDERGARTEN PAPER DOLLS* - Box (6020)
6066 *MARLO THOMAS AS "THAT GIRL"* - Box (4479)
6067 *KEWPIE-KINS IN KEWPIEVILLE* 1968 - Box (6088)
6068 *PAPER DOLLS WITH LACE-ON COSTUMES* (Janie, Sue and Nancy) 1955
6068 *PAPER DOLLS WITH LACE-ON COSTUMES* (Bunny, Linda and Carol)
6068 *PAPER DOLLS WITH LACE-ON COSTUMES* (Elaine, Michele and Carolyn)
6069 *THE FLYING NUN* 1968 - Box (5121)
6071 *PARTY PAPER DOLLS* 1973, date on box, 1969 on inside pages (4442)
6072 *MINI MOPPETS* 1969/1973 (4440)
6076 *WEDDING PARTY DOLLS* - Box (2749)
6078 *MOTHER AND DAUGHTER* 1963 - Box
6078 *TEEN BOUTIQUE* 1973 - Box (4260)
6079 *DARLING DOLLS WITH WAVY HAIR* 1957 - Box
6079 *SUSAN DEY* 1973 - Box (4218)
6081 *PENNY* (6091)
6082 *KISSY - 24" Tall* 1963 (1337)
6084 *SANDRA DEE PLAY KIT* 1960 (4413)
6088 *KEWPIE DOLLS* 1963 - Box
6091 *PENNY " THE PERSONALITY DOLL"* 1964 - Box
6092 *CONNIE DARLING AND HER DOLLY* 1964 - Box
6093 *PAPER DOLL BALLET* 1957 - Box
6093 *CONNIE DARLING AND HER DOLLY* - Box (6092)
6097 *SWEETHEART DOLLS WITH CLOTH DRESSES* 1957
6112 *STORY PRINCESS DOLLS* (Alene Dalton) 1957 - Box (2761)
6116 *POLLY AND MOLLY AND THEIR DOLLIES* - Box
6117 *KATHY AND SUE "JUST LIKE ME"* 1958 (They stand two feet high)
6128 *FOUR HI-HEEL STANDING DOLLS* 1959
6128 *BEAUTY QUEENS* (6128 Four Hi-Heel standing dolls)
6143 *KATHY AND SUE*, two "Just Like Me" Dolls (6117)
6155 *JULIA* - Box (4435)
6157 *THE PARTRIDGE FAMILY* 1972 - Box (5137)
6158 *BLUE BELLE PAPER DOLLS* - Box (6128)
6159 *PATCHWORK PAPER DOLLS* 1974 - Box (6059)
6160 *YOU ARE A DOLL* 1962 - Doll has a blank face for child's picture - Box
6168 *STANDING DOLLS WITH LACE-ON COSTUMES* 1969/1974 (6068)
6169 *3 DARLING DOLLS* 1964 - Box
6180 *TV FUN TIME* - Starring Woody Woodpecker - Box (1344)
6181 *ANNE, JUDY AND CAROL, DOLLS WITH WAVY HAIR* - Box (5180 and 5181 plus one new doll)
6189 *SIX STANDING DOLLS WITH LACE-ON COSTUMES* 1956 - Box
6194 *DARLING DOLLS WITH WAVY HAIR* 1957 - Box
6212 *PRESCHOOL PAPER DOLLS* (6020) - Box
6312 *PRESCHOOL PAPER DOLLS* (6020) - Box
6631 *BALLET PAPER DOLLS* 1964 (4431)
6632 *DOUBLE WEDDING* 1964 (4432)
6633 *UNITED NATIONS PAPER DOLLS* 1964 (4433)
6714 *EMERGENCY + 4* - Box - Stand-ups
6840 *PRESCHOOL PAPER DOLLS* - Box (6020)
6843 *SHARI LEWIS* (6060) - Box
6868 *PAPER DOLLS WITH LACE-ON COSTUMES* (6068 Carol, Bunny and Linda)
7890 *PROJECT GO* - Space stand-ups (3816)
7990 *PROJECT GO* - Space stand-ups (3816)
9518 *TIPPY TEEN* 1967/1972 Coloring/paper doll book (4612)
9546 *CHRISTMAS IN KEWPIEVILLE* 1962/1966 Coloring and paper doll book (Paper doll from #9553 with one new doll added)
9553 *THE KEWPIES* - A coloring and cut-out book 1962
9568 *THE STORY OF THE BALLET* - Coloring/paper doll book 1963/1964
9619 *ONCE UPON A WEDDING DAY* - Coloring/paper doll book
9646 *CHRISTMAS IN KEWPIEVILLE* 1962/66 - paper doll from #9553
9652 *THE KEWPIES* - A coloring and cut-out book (9553)
9653 *THE KEWPIES* - A coloring and cut-out book (9553)
9658 *KISSY* - Box (1337)
9668 *BALLET COLORING BOOK AND PAPER DOLL* (9568)
9856 *KATHY "JUST LIKE ME"* - 2 Ft. Tall 1958 (6117) - Box
9857 *SIX LACE-ON DOLLS* - Box (6189)
9859 *SHIRLEY TEMPLE PLAY KIT* 1958
9860 *DARLING DOLLS WITH REAL HAIR* - Box (6079)
9861 *PAPER DOLL SISTERS* - Box (6189)
9868 *PAPER DOLLS WITH LACE-ON COSTUMES* [   ]
9869 *SHIRLEY TEMPLE PLAY KIT* 1961 (9859)

The Samuel Lowe Publishing Company

Mr. Samuel Lowe was the founder and first president of the Samuel Lowe Publishing Company. He began his career in New York City working at the Henry Street Settlement House which compared with the Hull House in Chicago. Later, when Mr. Lowe moved to Racine, Wisconsin, he worked at the Central Association, a social service organization. His love for children and his interest in children's books prompted him in 1917 to take a job in Racine with the Western Printing and Lithographing Company (now Western Publishing Co.) to develop a line of children's books which eventually became incorporated into the Whitman line.

Twenty-three years after Samuel Lowe came to Western, he decided that it was "now or never" to try his hand at his own publishing company. So he left Western and started his own company a few miles away in Kenosha, Wisconsin. Among the companies early successes were their novelty books and novelty handle books consisting of several storybooks tied together with a ribbon or cord which then ran through a cardboard handle. A few years later, the company launched into their line of Bonnie Books which became very popular. These books are discussed in some detail near the end of the picture section for Lowe.

Mr. Lowe was president until his death in 1952. His wife, Edith Lowe, then became president and she has held this position up to the present. Mrs. Lowe, too, had worked for Western, starting there in 1924 and leaving when her husband left in 1940, the year the Lowe Company was founded. There are five Lowe sons; Samuel Jr., James, Jonathan, Peter and Richard. Three of the sons, Jonathan, Peter and Richard have held positions in the company.

Paper dolls were a big part of the Lowe Publishing Company's main line of children's books from the beginning. In the early years, they were drawn by such noted artists as Rachel Taft Dixon, Pelagie Doane, Doris and Marion Henderson and Fern Bisel Peat, and more recently by Queen Holden, George and Nan Pollard, Jeanne Voelz, Elsie Darien and Harriet Hentschel Struzenegger.

Since about the mid Fifties, many of the Lowe books were copyrighted by the James and Jonathan Company, an affiliated company which designed the books. Obviously, the company was named for two of the Lowe sons. Other trade names used at various times by the company were John Martins' House, Abbott Publishing, Angelus Publishing, Lolly Pop Books and Faircrest.

All Paper Dolls Pictured Are Copyrighted By The Samuel Lowe Company Unless Otherwise Stated.

Books Without Numbers

These books have been found with no identifying number.

CAPTAIN MARVEL 1942 - stand-ups
THE CAROL AND JERRY BOOK 1944 (same as book #148)
FOUR JOLLY FRIENDS 1944 (same as book #523-1)
JEAN AND HER TWIN BROTHER BOB (same as book #527)
BUSY DAYS (4207)
TEEN AGERS (1253 Prom)
PLAYTIME PALS (1283 and 1284)
LOLLYPOP KIDS (1252 Rockabye)
LET'S PLAY PAPER DOLLS (1045 Playtime Pals)
PRINCESS (1242)
THREE LITTLE SISTERS 1944 (same as book #525-1)
MARY ANN GROWS UP 1943 (same as book #1021)
BETSY DRESS A DOLL STORYBOOK 1964 (same as book #3946)
CINDY DRESS A DOLL STORYBOOK 1964 (same as book #3947)
WENDY DRESS A DOLL STORYBOOK 1964 (same as book #3945)
NANCY DRESS A DOLL STORYBOOK 1964 (same as book #3944)
VICTORY GIRLS - The following are small books.

ARLENE, THE AIRLINE HOSTESS (1045 Career Girls)
RUTH, OF THE STAGE DOOR CANTEEN (1048 Girls in Uniform)
FLORENCE, THE NURSE (1048 Girls in Uniform)
SYBIL, OF THE FIELD HOSPITAL (1048 Girls in Uniform)
ANN, THE SCHOOL TEACHER, on the ration board (1045 Career Girls)
EDITH, OF THE A.W.V.S. (1048 Girls in Uniform)
SANDRA, THE MOVIE STAR (1045 Career Girls)
ELEANOR OF THE O.C.D. (1048 Girls in Uniform)
BABS, THE AMULANCE DRIVER (1048 Girls in Uniform

Some of the different catalogs of the Lowe Company and a sheet of stationery with Bonnie Books letterhead.

#521

#522

#521

THE SAMUEL LOWE PICTURE SEC-
TION INCLUDES PAPER DOLLS
FROM THE JAMES AND JONATHAN
COMPANY, AND PAPER DOLLS US-
ING THE TRADE NAMES OF ABBOTT
PUBLISHING AND JOHN MARTINS'
HOUSE.

521 *LITTLE COUSINS* 1940. $5.00

521 *TWINKLE TWINS - 4 YEARS OLD* 1944 (date in Lowe
records). $5.00

522 *TWINKLE TWINS - 10 YEARS OLD* 1944 (date in Lowe
records). $5.00

521A *PLAYMATES* 1940. $5.00

A cut set of the dolls from
PLAYMATES #521A.

523 *BAB AND HER DOLL FURNITURE*
1943. $5.00

#521A

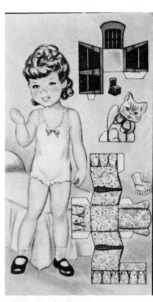

#523 Inside front cover.

523 *FARMER FRED* 1943. $5.00

Farmer Fred #523 Inside front cover.

Courtesy of Virginia Crossley.

523 *JANIE AND HER DOLL* 1943. $5.00

#523 Inside front cover. Janie and her doll.

Courtesy of Virginia Crossley.

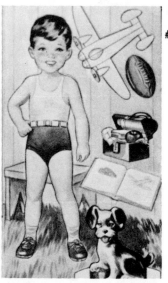

523 *TOM AND HIS TOYS* 1943. $5.00

#523 Inside front cover. Tom and His Toys

Courtesy of Virginia Crossley.

523 *MARY AND HER TOYS* 1943. $5.00

#523 Inside front cover. Mary and Her Toys.

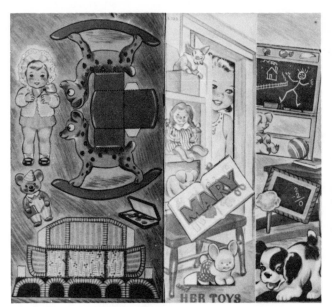

Copyright Metro-Goldwyn-Mayer, Inc.

955 *DR. KILDARE PLAY BOOK.* $3.00

#955 Inside pages of paper doll.

Courtesy of Audrey Sepponen.

958 *CAREER GIRLS* 1950 (date in Lowe records). $10.00

968 *SQUARE DANCE* 1950 (date in Lowe records). $5.00

#1021 Inside front cover.

#1021 Inside back cover.

Courtesy of Virginia Crossley.

1021 *THE BABY SHOW* 1940. $20.00

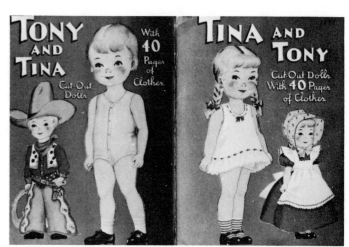

990 *TV TAP STARS* 1952 (date in Lowe records). $6.00

1022 *TINA AND TONY* 1940. $15.00

Courtesy of Emma Terry.

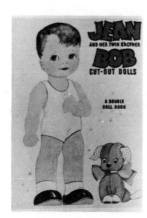

Courtesy of Virginia Crossley.

1023 *SALLY AND DICK, BOB AND JEAN* 1940 A Double Doll Book. $20.00

#1023 Inside back cover.

#1023 Inside front cover.

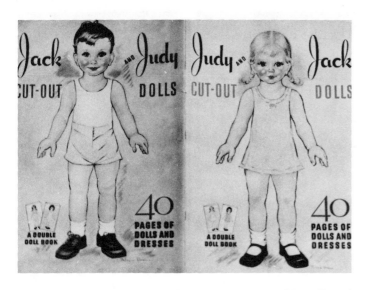

1024 *JUDY AND JACK, PEG AND BILL* 1940 A Double Doll Book. $25.00

#1024 Inside front and back cover.

Courtesy of Audrey Sepponen.

1024 *POLLY PATCHWORK AND HER FRIENDS* 1941. $15.00

Courtesy of Shirley Hedge.

1027 *IN OUR BACKYARD* 1941. $15.00

Courtesy of Betsy Slap.

1025 *TURNABOUT DOLLS* 1943. $15.00

#1025 Reverse side of front and back covers Turnabout Dolls.

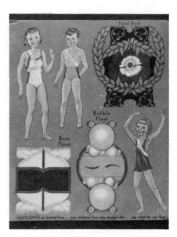

1026 *PAPER DOLLS' BEAUTY CONTEST* With Floats, Costumes
Prizes 1941. $20.00

Courtesy of Virginia Crossley.

1026 *DUDE RANCH* 1943 Turnabout paper dolls. $10.00

#1026 Reverse sides of front and back covers Dude Ranch.

Courtesy of Audrey Sepponen.

1028 *PLAYHOUSE PAPER DOLLS* 1941 This book contains reversible clothes. $15.00

#1028 Inside front cover.

#1028 Inside back cover.

Courtesy of Virginia Crossley.

#1028 Reverse of front cover.

#1028 Reverse of back cover

1028 *GIRLS IN THE WAR* 1943 Turnabout doll book. $15.00

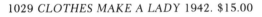

Courtesy of Mrs. Samuel Lowe.

#1029 Inside front cover.

1029 *CLOTHES MAKE A LADY* 1942. $15.00

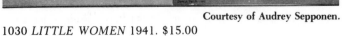

Courtesy of Audrey Sepponen.

Courtesy of Mrs. Samuel Lowe.

1030 *LITTLE WOMEN* 1941. $15.00

1044 *BLUE FEATHER INDIAN* 1944 Silver Cloud Indian on back cover. (Date from Lowe records). $20.00

Courtesy of Audrey Sepponen.

1030 *THE FIVE LITTLE PEPPERS* 1941. $15.00

Courtesy of Audrey Sepponen.

1030 *ANNIE LAURIE* 1941. $15.00

Courtesy of Audrey Sepponen.

1040 *KING OF SWING AND QUEEN OF SONG* 1942 Benny Goodman and Peggy Lee. Turnabout Doll Book. $60.00 & up.

#1040 Reverse side of front cover.

#1040 Reverse side of back cover.

Courtesy of Audrey Sepponen.

1041 *GLENN MILLER, MARION HUTTON* 1942 Turnabout Doll Book. $60.00 & up.

#1041 Reverse side of front cover.   #1041 Reverse side of back cover.

Courtesy of Mrs. Samuel Lowe.

1042 *JUNIOR PROM* 1942. $12.00

1043 *BETTY BO-PEEP* 1942 (Billy Boy Blue on back cover). $20.00

Courtesy of Betsy Slap.

1025 *THE 8 AGES OF JUDY* 1941. $35.00

1043 *THE BRIDE DOLL* 1946. $10.00

1025 *THE 8 AGES OF JUDY*, Inside pages.

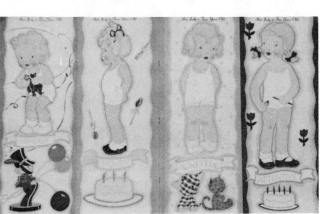

1042 *PAT THE "STAND-UP" DOLL* 1946 (date in Lowe records). $12.00

Courtesy of Virginia Crossley.

1044 *ME AND MIMI* 1942 (Includes a small paper doll book of Mimi). $15.00

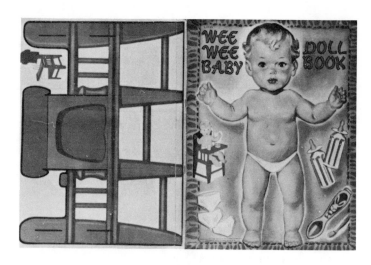

1045 *WEE WEE BABY DOLL BOOK* 1945. $15.00

1045 *CAREER GIRLS* 1942. $15.00 Courtesy of Mrs. Samuel Lowe.

1045 *PLAYTIME PALS* 1946. $5.00

Courtesy of Audrey Sepponen.

1046 *CLOTHES CRAZY* 1945 (date in Lowe records). $10.00

Courtesy of Mrs. Samuel Lowe.

1048 *GIRLS IN UNIFORM* 1942. $15.00

Courtesy of Audrey Sepponen.

1048 *THE TURNABOUTS DOLL BOOK* 1943. $10.00

1049 *HOLLYWOOD PERSONALITIES* 1941. $60.00 & up.

Courtesy of Betsy Slap.

1049 *LOLLYPOP CROWD* 1945 (date in Lowe records). $15.00

Courtesy of Audrey Sepponen.

1056 *DOWN ON THE FARM.* $10.00

1057 *PLAYHOUSE PAPER DOLLS* 1947 (date in Lowe records). This book was patterned after the earlier book of *PLAYHOUSE* #1028. For this book new dolls and clothes were drawn. $8.00

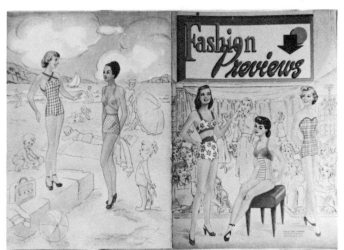

Courtesy of Mrs. Samuel Lowe.

1246 *FASHION PREVIEWS* 1949. $10.00

1074 *TOM THE AVIATOR* 1941. $8.00

Courtesy of Virginia Crossley.

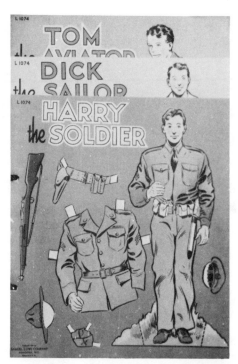

Courtesy of Virginia Crossley.

These three books are tied together to sell as one book.

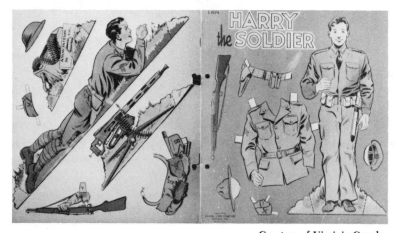

1074 *HARRY THE SOLDIER* 1941. $8.00

Courtesy of Virginia Crossley.

Courtesy of Mrs. Samuel Lowe.

1077 *LITTLE BEAR TO DRESS* 1942. $10.00

1077 *LITTLE DOG TO DRESS* 1942. $10.00

1077 *LITTLE PIG TO DRESS* 1942. $10.00

1077 *LITTLE KITTEN TO DRESS* 1942. $10.00

These four books tied together and sold as one book. Date is from Lowe catalog.

1074 *DICK THE SAILOR* 1941. $8.00

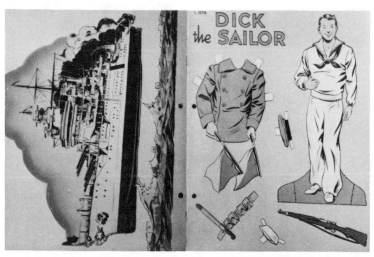

Courtesy of Virginia Crossley.

#1242 Inside front cover.

1242 *CINDERELLA STEPS OUT* 1948. $10.00

Courtesy of Audrey Sepponen.

1248 *LET'S PLAY HOUSE* Furniture and Dolls with dresses. The furniture in this book originated with *DOLL HOUSE* #7502, a box set published in 1943. There is no date on this book, but it is shown in the 1949 catalog. $4.00

Courtesy of Mrs. Samuel Lowe.

1251 *NEW TONI HAIR-DO DRESS-UP DOLLS* 1951. $15.00

1252 *ROCKABYE BABIES* 1952 (date in Lowe records). $7.00

1253 *PROM HOME PERMANENT* 1952. $10.00

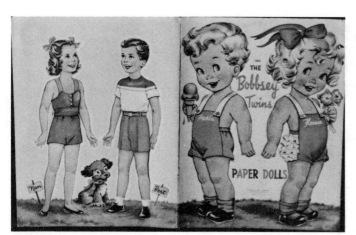

1254 *THE BOBBSEY TWINS* 1952 (date in Lowe records). $10.00

Courtesy of Betsy Slap.

1283 *CUDDLES AND RAGS* 1950 (date in Lowe records). $10.00

Courtesy of Mrs. Samuel Lowe.

1284 *TONI HAIR-DO CUT-OUT DOLLS* 1950. $15.00

1286 *COWBOYS AND COWGIRLS* 1950 (date in Lowe records). $5.00

1829 *PLAYMATES* 1961 (date in Lowe records). $2.00

1831 *LOLLIPOP KIDS* 1961 (date in Lowe records). $2.00

#1829 is a redrawn book from *FUN ON THE FARM* #1056 and #1831 is from *LOLLIPOP CROWD* #1049. They are shown here because some of these dolls are later used in reprints of their own; for example the #3910 Dressmaker sets.

#1829

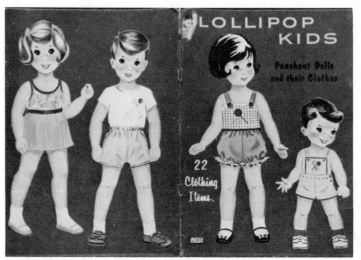

#1831

#2742 School Children.

1832 *LOTS OF DOLLS* 1961 (date in Lowe records).
This book uses clothes from #1057 *PLAYHOUSE*, but the dolls are completely new. They do not use the figures of the *PLAYHOUSE* dolls at all. In 1963 *SCHOOL CHILDREN* #2742 used these new dolls and new clothes were drawn. All later reprints use the new clothes from *SCHOOL CHILDREN* and the dolls from this book of *LOTS OF DOLLS*. $2.00

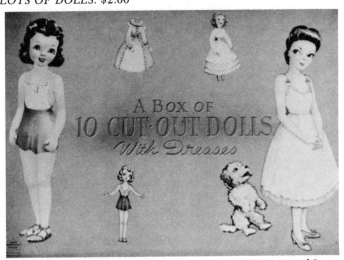

Courtesy of Mrs. Samuel Lowe.

1842 *A BOX OF 10 CUT-OUT DOLLS WITH DRESSES.*
This beautiful box set of ten paper dolls was drawn by Helen Page. Each doll has her own little folder complete with clothes and accessories. The folders are of a fine quality paper which accentuates the delicate pastels used by the artist. In addition to the dolls in the folders, the same dolls were also printed on sheets of cardboard. This set was published using one of the Lowe Company trade marks - JOHN MARTIN'S HOUSE and is in the 1947 catalog. $50.00

1885 *LITTLE DRESSMAKER DOLL BOOK - PATTY* 1966. $1.00

1886 *LITTLE DRESSMAKER DOLL BOOK - LUCY* 1966. $1.00

1887 *LITTLE DRESSMAKER DOLL BOOK - JANIE* 1966. $1.00

2404 *THREE LITTLE MAIDS FROM SCHOOL ARE WE* 1957. $4.00

From Lowe catalog.

#2110 Inside center pages of paper dolls. **Courtesy of Audrey Sepponen.** 2110 *SANTA'S BAND* 1962 Christmas Punch-out Book. $2.00

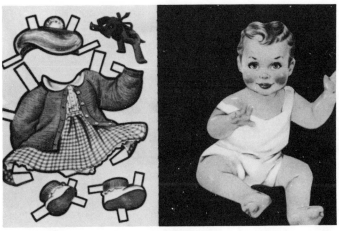

#2403 Doll and one of the pages of clothes.

Courtesy of Mrs. Samuel Lowe.

2411 *PATIENCE AND PRUDENCE* 1957. $7.00

2405 *JANET LEIGH* 1957. $25.00

2403 *BABY DOLL*
1957. $4.00

Copyright Leigh-Mor, Inc. Courtesy of Audrey Sepponen.

Copyright Lear Music Corp.

2406 *PATTI PAGE* 1957. $25.00

2407 *THE BOB CUMMINGS FASHION MODELS* 1957. $30.00

Courtesy of Emma Terry.

2424 KEEPSAKE FOLIO - TRUDY DOLL
1964. $5.00

2422 KEEPSAKE FOLIO - MIMI DOLL
1964. $5.00

2423 KEEPSAKE FOLIO - EMILY DOLL
1964. $5.00

2483 JUNIOR MISSES 1958
Junior Misses was reprinted comany times using different titles. One reprint is ARCHIES GIRLS which uses three of the dolls and clothes from Junior Misses. For that book the dolls were redrawn. $6.00

#2483 A folder type book that opens from the middle. **Courtesy of Virginia Crossley.**

#2483 Outside of folder and dolls.

2488 *PATTI PAGE* 1958. $25.00

2493 *BRIDE AND GROOM DOLLS* 1959. $5.00

Courtesy of Mrs. Samuel Lowe.

Courtesy of Mrs. Samuel Lowe.

2523 *KAY AND KIM WITH CLOTHES TO TRIM* 1956 With colored gummed pages to complete dresses. $4.00

2560 *THE HONEYMOONERS* 1956. $25.00

2561 *GOLDILOCKS AND THE THREE BEARS* 1955. $6.00

2562 *HERE COMES THE BRIDE* 1955. $5.00

Courtesy of Mrs. Samuel Lowe.
2563 *HIS AND HERS - THE GUEST TOWEL DOLLS* 1955. $5.00

2574 *BETSY'S SUNDAY BEST* 1955 (date in Lowe records). $3.00

#2569

Courtesy of Mrs. Samuel Lowe.

#2585

2569 *ROSEMARY CLOONEY* 1956. $35.00

2585 *GLORIA'S MAKE-UP* 1952 (date in Lowe records).
The paper doll from Gloria's Make-Up was redrawn in 1953 and became Rosemary Clooney! Six of eight pages of clothes from Gloria were retained in the Rosemary Clooney books. $15.00

2713 *MOPSY AND POPSY* 1971. $1.00

2610 *SALLY'S DRESS A DOLL STORYBOOK* 1952 (date in Lowe records). $3.00

2714 *DOLLIES GO 'ROUND THE WORLD* 1971. $1.00

Courtesy of Virginia Crossley.

2717 *WHEN WE GROW UP* 1971. $1.00

#2718

#2721

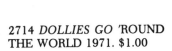

#2720

2718 *HERE COMES THE BRIDE* 1971. $1.00

2720 *DRESS ANNABELLE* 1972. $1.00

2721 *DOLL FRIENDS* 1972. $1.00

2722 *LITTLE DOLLS* 1972. $1.00

2723 *A HOUSE FULL OF DOLLS AND CLOTHES* 1972. $1.00

2724 *NOW AND THEN PAPER DOLLS* 1973. $1.00

2725 *THE HAPPY FAMILY* 1973. $1.00

Courtesy of Audrey Sepponen.

2743 *TWO TEENS* 1963. $1.00

2749 *BABY ANNE SMILES AND CRYS* 1964. $4.00

2750 *ELIZABETH* Alive - Like Dolly 1963. $4.00

2751 *BONNIE* Alive - Like Dolly 1963. $4.00

Courtesy of Audrey Sepponen.

2751 *BIG DOLL BETTY* 1960. $2.00

#2760

2760 *DOTTY DOLL BOOK* 1968. New doll drawn in the figure of Mimi #3905. Clothes are from Mimi #2743. $1.00

2762 *VICKY* 1967. Doll is new, clothes from Bonnie #2751. $3.00

2763 *DOLLY GETS LOTS OF NEW CLOTHES* 1967. Doll is new, clothes from Elizabeth #2750. $3.00

Books #2760, #2762 and #2763 are not original books but are shown here because they have reprints of their own.

#2762

#2763

2764 *PIXIE DOLL AND PUP* 1968. $3.00

2766 *FRONT AND BACK DOLLS AND DRESSES* 1964. $1.00

2784 *LITTLE GIRLS* 1969. $1.00

2785 *SALLY, SUE AND SHERRY* 1969. $1.00

2906 *BETSY DRESS A DOLL STORYBOOK* 1960. Each page a different outfit. $2.00
2915 *WENDY DRESS A DOLL STORYBOOK* 1959. Each page a different outfit. $2.00

3727 *JEANNIE AND GENE* 1975. $1.00

3730 *POLLY PAL* 1976. $1.00

2904 *SEW-ON SHERRY ANN'S CLOTHES* 1960. $2.00

Picture courtesy of the Lowe Company.

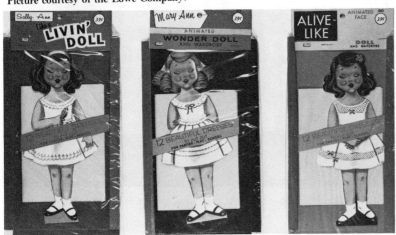

Courtesy of Samuel Lowe Company.

3903 *SALLY ANN* - like a Livin' Doll - Animated face (in 1960 catalog). $1.00

3903 *MARY ANN* - Animated Wonder Doll (in 1960 catalog). $1.00

3903 *BETTY ANN* - Alive-like Animated Face (in 1960 catalog). $1.00

3905 *MIMI FROM PAREE* 1960. $2.00

3921 *PATTI DOLL BOOK* 1961. New doll, clothes come from the three #3903 dolls. This book is shown here even though not a true original as it has reprints of its own. $2.00

4171 *GABBY HAYES* 1954 Tall Tales for Little Folks A Bonnie Jack-in-the-Box Book. $5.00

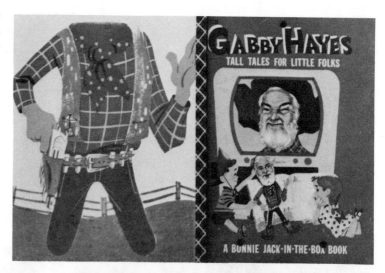

Courtesy of Audrey Sepponen.
3947 *CINDY* 1964 Storybook Doll. $3.00

#4171 Inside front cover showing doll and pages of the story with one of the outfits.

4207 *PENNY'S PARTY* 1952 A Paper Doll Story Book [Bonnie Book]. $2.00

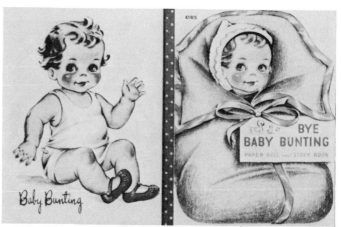

4219 *BYE BABY BUNTING* 1953. Paper Doll and Story Book [Bonnie Book type of book]. $2.00

The Samuel Lowe Company Bonnie Books

The Bonnie Books published by the Lowe Company are some of the most unique storybooks ever made. They are small books, 8 x 6½ inches, and included Pop-up books, Television books with a TV screen that changes pictures as a dial is turned, Push Along books of trains, fire engines, etc., with wheels that turn, books of paper dolls and other cut out books, containing scissors attached to the cover. Also part of the Bonnie Book line were books with boxes of crayons or paint sets attached. Another novelty is a baby's book with a rattle attached to the front cover. Then there are Bonnie spinner game books, progressive games with the spinner showing through the pages as the game progressed, and Bonnie Merry-Go-Round books which when opened, form individual stage-like scenes portraying the characters and scenery of the story. There are even Bonnie Books with jigsaw puzzles inside, and books of other games and puzzles. The list is endless. Each new catalog illustrated new and unusual Bonnie Books.

#4263   #4264

4263 *SHERLOCK BONES* - and his many disquises 1955. [Bonnie Book]. $1.00

4264 *DOLLY GOES ROUND THE WORLD* 1955 [Bonnie Book]. This is a Jiggle-head book with costumes on each page. The doll's head shows through the front cover of the Jiggle-head books. $1.00

#4266 $1.00   #4265

4265 *BILLY BOY* 1953 (also 1955) Jack-in-the-book [Bonnie Book].

4266 *BETTY PLAYS LADY* 1953 Jack-in-the-book [Bonnie Book].

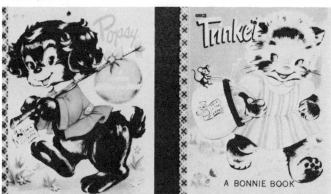

#4267   #4268

4267 *POPSY - Jack-in-the-book* 1953 [Bonnie Book]. $1.00

4268 *TRINKET - Jack-in-the-book* 1953 [Bonnie Book]. $1.00

#4281   #4282

4281 *CIRCUS TIME* 1952 Jack-in-the-book [Bonnie Book]. $1.00

4282 *LITTLE SUGAR BEAR* 1952 Jack-in-the-book [Bonnie Book].

4284 *COOKIE THE RABBIT* 1952 Jack-in-the-book [Bonnie Book].

4343 *CAPTAIN BIG BILL* 1956 Jack-in-the-book [Bonnie Book].

4283 *DOLLY TAKES A TRIP* 1952 Jack-in-the-book [Bonnie Book]. $1.00

#4299   #4298   #4344   #4345

4298 *JUNGLETOWN JAMBOREE* Spin-dial book [Bonnie Book].   4344 *ALFIE* 1956 Jack-in-the-book [Bonnie Book]. $1.00
4299 *MASQUERADE PARTY* 1955 Spin-dial book [Bonnie Book].   4345 *TIMMY* 1956 Jack-in-the-book [Bonnie Book]. $1.00
$1.00

4913 *AIRLINE STEWARDESS* 1957. $5.00   5901 *SUZY* 1961 Alive-Like Face Doll Book. $2.00

5908 *MOLLY DOLLY* 1962 Doll and clothes new, except for four
outfits that come from Mimi #3905. $2.00

9986 *KATHY 30 INCH STAND-UP DOLL* 1962. $15.00
Courtesy of Samuel Lowe Company.

8902 *LACE AND DRESS PUPPY* 1975. $2.00

8903 *LACE AND DRESS KITTY* 1975. $2.00

Courtesy of Samuel Lowe Company.

9045 *TWO LITTLE GIRLS - BIG BIG DOLL BOOK* 1964. Dolls new, clothes from #2904 and #2915. Not a completely original book, but is shown here because this book has reprints of its own. $15.00

9041 *PEGGY AND PETER* 1962 Big, Big Doll Book. $18.00

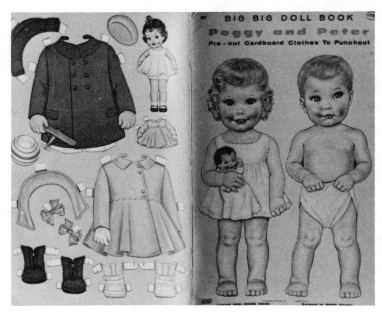

9118 *BETSY* 1964 - Box (Doll has animated mouth). $15.00

Picture from Lowe Catalog.

Doll and clothes from #6918, same as #9118 except doll does not have animated mouth.

9985 *CECELIA MY KISSIN' COUSIN* -30 inches tall 1960. $15.00

9301 *JACK* 1963. $15.00

9302 *JILL* 1963. $15.00

Courtesy of Samuel Lowe Company.

Courtesy of Samuel Lowe Company.

Courtesy of Samuel Lowe Company.

List of Paper Dolls Published by the Samuel Lowe Company

This list contains all original and reprint books and box sets published by the Samuel Lowe Company plus those published under other Lowe Company trade names as Abbott, James and Jonathan, Bonnie Books and John Martin's House. Also included are a few books that were made for Sears and the Bestmaid Company.

Reprints will have the number of the original book it is derived from in parenthesis following the title. Brackets without any numbers indicate a reprint where the original is nor definitely known. It should be remembered that the reprint is not always the same as the original. For example, sometimes only one or two dolls of the original book were used. Other examples of how reprints may differ from the original are mentioned on page 4.

8 *PLAYROOM PAPER DOLLS* - Box of five books all dated 1944. #523-1 *FOUR JOLLY FRIENDS*, #523-2 *SUSIE AND BETTY*, #525-1 *THREE LITTLE SISTERS*, #525-2 *STAND-OUT DOLLS*, #526-1 *BABY CUT-OUTS* and sometimes a sixth book would be substituted - #526-2 *FOUR PLAYMATES*.

L-24 *PLAYROOM PAPER DOLLS* - Box of five books all numbered L523 -*TOM, MARY, FRED, BAB AND JANIE*.

58 *VICTORY GIRLS* - Box (1048 Girls in Uniform)

78 *PLAYROOM PAPER DOLLS* - Box of five assorted paper doll books from the 1940's. Books varied as to titles available in stock.

123 *PLAYMATES* (1025 Turnabout Dolls)

124 *FOUR CUT-OUT DOLLS* - Nancy, Judy, Susan, Betty 1942 (1025 - 8 Ages of Judy)

125 *PLAYGROUND* 1944 (1025 Turnabout Dolls)

125 *FOUR PLAYMATE CUT-OUT DOLLS* (1021 Baby Show)

126 *BIG ROUND-UP* (1026 Dude Ranch)

L126 *DUDE RANCH* (1026)

127 *SALLY AND HER TWIN BROTHER DICK* 1944 (1023)

127 *THE PLAYTIME TWINS* (1023 Sally, Dick, Bob and Jean)

128 *THE TWINS BOB AND JEAN* 1944 (1023)

128 *ANN AND BETTY* (521A and 521 Little Cousins)

129 *CLOTHES MAKE A LADY* (   )

130 *BETTY, JANE AND DICK* 1943 (1023 Sally, Dick, etc. and 1022 Tina and Tony)

131 *TINA AND TONY* (1022)

132 *CUT-OUT KIDS* (   )

132 *MY BIG DOLLS* (   )

132 *PLAYGROUND* (   )

133 *CUT-OUT FUN* (   )

133 *MY BIG DOLLS* 1944 (1025 Turnabout Dolls)

142 *JUDY AND MARY* (1025 Turnabout Dolls)

142 *JUNIOR PROM* 1942 (1042)

143 *PEGGY AND CAROL* (1025 Turnabout Dolls)

143 *BETTY BO-PEEP* (1043)

L144 *ME AND MIMI* 1942 (1044)

144 *BLUE FEATHER - SILVER CLOUD* (1044)

145 *TEN LITTLE PLAYMATES* 1944 (521A)

145 *GIRLS IN UNIFORM* 1943 (1048)

146 *CUT-OUT DOLLS FOR FUN AND PLAY* (521 Little Cousins)

148 *CAROL AND JERRY* 1944 (1022 Tina and Tony)

148 *THE OUTDOOR GIRLS* (1048 The Turnabouts)

149 *SUE AND TOM* 1944 (1022 Tina and Tony)

228 *PETER AND PRUE* - Box (1021 Baby Show)

294 *NINE DOLL BOX* (521A)

313 *ROSEMARY CLOONEY* - Coloring book with paper dolls on covers, no outfits.

521 *LITTLE COUSINS* 1940

521 *TWINKLE TWINS 4 YEARS OLD* 1944 (date in Lowe records)

521 *SUNBONNET SUE* 1943 (1029)

521A *PLAYMATES* 1940

522 *TWINKLE TWINS 10 YEARS OLD* 1944 (date in Lowe records)

522 *SONNY AND SUE* 1940 (1022 Tina and Tony)

522 *DEBS, A PRESSED BOARD DOLL* (1045 Career Girls)

522 *GROWN-UPS* 1943 (1045 Career Girls)

523 *PLAYROOM DOLLS* - Box which contained the following five books - #523 *TOM AND HIS TOYS* 1943; #523 *BAB AND HER FURNITURE* 1943; #523 *JANIE AND HER DOLL* 1943; #523 *MARY AND HER TOYS* 1943; #523 *FARMER FRED* 1943.

523 *PEG AND BILL* 1941 (1024)

523 *JUDY AND JACK* 1941 (1024)

523-1 *FOUR JOLLY FRIENDS* 1944 (521A)

523-2 *SUSIE AND BETTY* 1944 (521 Little Cousins)

523-3 *THREE LITTLE SISTERS AND THEIR CLOTHES* (521A) and (521 Little Cousins)

524 *BETSY AND BILL* 1943 (1021 Baby Show)

524 *CUT-OUT BOOK WITH REAL WOOD DOLL* (521A)

525   *PATTY AND PETE* 1941 (1022 Tina and Tony)
525   *STAND-OUT DOLLS* 1944 (521 Little Cousins)
525-1   *THREE LITTLE SISTERS* 1944 (521A) and (521 Little Cousin)
525-2   *STAND-OUT PAPER DOLLS* 1944 (521A) and (521 Little Cousins)
526   *CUT-OUT BOOK WITH REAL WOOD DOLL* (521A)
526   *EIGHT LITTLE PLAYMATES* 1944 (1021 Baby Show)
526-1   *BABY CUT-OUT DOLLS* 1944 (1021 Baby Show)
526-2   *FOUR PLAYMATES* 1944 (1021 Baby Show)
527   *SALLY AND HER TWIN BROTHER DICK* 1943 (1023)
527   *JEAN AND HER BROTHER BOB* (1023)
528   *PETER AND PRUE* 1942 (1021 Baby Show)
528   *BETSY AND BILL* 1942 (1021 Baby Show)
528   *BETSY AND BILL* 1943 (1021 Baby Show)
529   *WAR GIRLS* 1943 (1048 Girls in Uniform)
536   *MODEL PLANES* 1943 - stand-ups
537   *COWBOY CUT-OUT BOOK* 1943 - stand-ups
613   *DOLL HOUSE DOLLIES* 1966 (1832 Lots of Dolls)
621   *WORLD FAMOUS KISSIN COUSIN* - Life Size Stand-up Doll 1967 (9985)
622   *KATHY* - Life Size Doll 1967 (9986)
724   *A BOX OF CUT-OUT DOLL BOOKS* 1944 - Four books - #521A *PLAYMATES*, #523-1 *FOUR JOLLY FRIENDS*, #525-1 *THREE LITTLE SISTERS* and #526-2 *FOUR PLAYMATES*. Other books may have been substituted.
730   *MOPSY AND POPSY* - Box 1972 (2713)
731   *JANE AND JILL* - Box 1972 (2784 Little Girls)
731   *KITTY AND PUPPY LACE-ON* 1975 - Box (8902 and 8903)
732   *DRESSMAKERS DOLL SET* 1972 - Box (1829 Playmates and 1831 Lollipop Kids)
733   *DOTTY DOLLY LACE-ON DOLL* 1972 - Box (2760)
937   *BABY SITTER* (1025 Turnabout)
945   *DRESS ALIKE* (1283)
945   *BABY SITTER* (1025 Turnabout) and (1046 Clothes Crazy)
946   *DOWN ON THE FARM* (1056)
946   *DANCE TEAM* (990)
947   *SWEET SIXTEEN - VIVIAN, RUTH AND PEGGY* (1253 Prom)
948   *SATURDAY NIGHT BARN DANCE* (968)
948   *SUNNY AND SUE* (1049 Lollipop) and (1252 Rockabye)
949   *LITTLE NEIGHBOR* (1254 Bobbsey)
950   *BROTHER AND SISTER* (521 and 522 Twinkle Twins)
950   *CAMPUS QUEENS* (1046 Clothes Crazy)
951   *JAMBOREE DOLLS* (968)
951   *COUNTRY COUSINS* (1056)
952   *WEDDING PARTY* (1043)
952   *PROM DATE* (1046 Clothes Crazy)
953   *SWING YOUR PARTNERS* (968)
953   *HOLLYWOOD DOLLS* (1246)
954   *BIG SISTERS IN PARIS* (958 Career Girls)
954   *COWGIRLS* (1026 Dude Ranch)
955   *DR. KILDARE PLAY BOOK* (has paper doll)
955   *TV STYLE SHOW* (1246)
958   *CAREER GIRLS* 1950 (date in Lowe records)
958   *PARTY DOLLS* (990)
959   *DOLLY AND ME* (1284)
960   *TONI HAIR-DO CUT-OUT DOLLS* 1950 (1284)
961   *TV STAR TIME* (990)
962   *CAMPUS QUEENS* (1253 Prom)
963   *TWINKLE TOTS* (1252 Rockabye) and (1049 Lollypop)
964   *CUDDLES AND RAGS* (1283)
965   *MY FAVORITE DOLL BOOK* (1254)-[Bobbsey]
968   *SQUARE DANCE* 1950 (date in Lowe records)
969   *HOLLYWOOD DOLLS* (1246)
970   *JUDY AND HER FRIENDS* - 5 dolls with clothes to be colored (1046)-[Clothes Crazy]
971   *COWGIRLS* (1026)-[Dude Ranch]
972   *FAIRGROUND* (1049)-[Lollypop]
973   *BOARDWALK* (522 and 521)-[Twinkle Twins]
975   *BOARDWALK* (522 and 521)-[Twinkle Twins]
977   *BOARDWALK* (522 and 521)-[Twinkle Twins]
978   *POLKA PARTY* (968)
980   *BIG SISTER* (958)-[Career Girls]
981   *CAMPUS QUEENS* (1046)-[Clothes Crazy]
982   *COWGIRLS* (1026)-[Dude Ranch]
983   *HOLLYWOOD DOLLS* (958)-[Career Girls]
984   *JAMBOREE DOLL BOOK* (968)
985   *WEDDING PARTY* (1043)
986   *MODELS DOLL BOOK* (1246)
988   *LOOK-ALIKE CUT-OUT DOLLS* (1284)
989   *NORA DRAKE* 1952 (958)-[Career Girls]
990   *TV TAP STARS* 1952 (date in Lowe records)
1009   *FASHION MODELS* (2407)
1010   *TWINS* - Baby Dolls, Jane and Jill (4219)
1011   *TEEN-AGE DOLLS* (2483)
1012   *SISTER DOLLS* - Sherry and Nancy (2411)
1013   *HONEYMOON DOLLS* (2493)
1014   *MARY JANE* (1283)
1015   *BABY SITTER* (1025)-[Turnabout] and (1046)-[Clothes Crazy]
1016   *YOUNG COUPLE* (2407)
1021   *MARY ANN GROWS UP* 1943 (1025)-[8 Ages of Judy]
1021   *BABY SHOW* - 25 dolls 1940
1022   *TINA AND TONY* 1940
1022   *CLOTHES MAKE A LADY* 1942 (1044)-[Mimi]

1023   *SALLY AND DICK, BOB AND JEAN* 1940
1023   *PRESSED BOARD DOLLS* 1942 (1048)-[Girls in Uniform]
1024   *JUDY AND JACK, PEG AND BILL* 1941
1024   *POLLY PATCHWORK AND HER FRIENDS* 1941
1024   *BUMPITY BESS* 1943 (1022)-[Tina and Tony]
1025   *THE 8 AGES OF JUDY* 1941
1025   *TURNABOUT DOLLS* 1943
1026   *BEAUTY CONTEST* 1941
1026   *DUDE RANCH*, Turnabout paper dolls 1943
1027   *THE TURNABOUT TWINS* 1943 (1023)-[Sally, Dick, Bob and Jean]
1027   *IN OUR BACKYARD* 1941
1028   *PLAYHOUSE PAPER DOLLS* 1941
1028   *GIRLS IN THE WAR*, Turnabout Doll Book 1943
1029   *CLOTHES MAKE A LADY* 1942
1030   *LITTLE WOMEN* 1941, *FIVE LITTLE PEPPERS* 1941, *ANNIE LAURIE* 1941 - These are three separate books, but are tied together and sold as one book.
1031   *DOLL PACKET* - un-named dolls (4913)
1031   *DOLL PACKET* - un-named doll (2585)
1032   *DOLL PACKET* - 3 dolls (2404)
1032   *DOLL PACKET* - (2407)
1032   *DOLL PACKET* - Peggy (1253)-[Prom]
1033   *DOLL PACKET* - (2405)
1034   *DOLL PACKET* - Prudence and Patience (2411)
1034   *DOLL PACKET* - (2406)
1035   *DOLL PACKET* - (2407)
1035   *DOLL PACKET* - Ruth and Vivian (1253)-[Prom]
1036   *DOLL PACKET* - (1283)
1036   *DOLL PACKET* - Prudence and Patience (2411)
1040   *KING OF SWING* - Benny Goodman and Peggy Lee 1942
1040   *BABY BUNTING* - Two versions, paper dolls from #1021 Baby Show or #1045 Wee Wee Baby.
1040   *GIRL AND BOY* (2407)
1041   *GLEN MILLER* 1942
1041   *CUTIE DOLL* (1283)
1041   *CUT-ME OUT PAPER DOLLS* - Bab, Fred, Tom, Mary and Janie (523)
1042   *JUNIOR PROM* 1942
1042   *SALLY THE STANDING DOLL* (1042)-[Pat]
1042   *PAT THE STAND-UP DOLL* - 1946 (date in Lowe records)
1042   *HOLLYWOOD GLAMOUR* (2407)
1042   *JUDY AND MARY* (1025)-[Turnabout]
1043   *BETTY BO PEEP* - Billy Boy Blue 1942
1043   *THE BRIDE DOLL* 1946
1043   *PEGGY AND CAROL* - Two Big Dolls (1025)-[Turnabout]
1043   *THREE LITTLE MAIDS FROM SCHOOL* (2404)
1044   *ME AND MIMI* 1942
1044   *BRIDE DOLL BOOK* (2493)
1044   *BLUE FEATHER* - Silver Cloud - 1944 (date in Lowe records)
1044   *COLLEGE GIRLS* 1946 (date in Lowe records) (1046)-[Clothes Crazy]
1045   *CAREER GIRLS* 1942
1045   *WEE WEE BABY* 1945
1045   *PLAYTIME PALS* 1946
1045   *GOING PLACES WITH MARY AND BILL* (2563)
1046   *FUZZY HEADS* 1942 (1029 for the girl) and (1043 Betty Bo Peep, for the boy)
1046   *CLOTHES CRAZY* 1945 - (date in Lowe records)
1047   *NANCY AND JUDY* 1942 - Susan and Betty on back cover. (1025 8 Ages of Judy)
1047   *ROMANCE* (1842 - Box of 10 Cut-out Dolls)
1047   *MAID OF BOARD* (1024 Judy and Jack, etc)
1048   *THE TURNABOUTS* 1943
1048   *GIRLS IN UNIFORM* 1942
1048   *LOTS OF DOLLS* (1025 Turnabout)
1049   *HOLLYWOOD PERSONALITIES* 1941
1049   *LOLLYPOP CROWD* 1945 - (date in Lowe records)
1051   *MERRY GO ROUND*, in 1962 catalog - stand-ups
1052   *FIRE DEPARTMENT*, in 1962 catalog - stand-ups
1053   *OUR TOWN*, in 1962 catalog - stand-ups
1053   *HERE COMES THE BRIDE* (1043)
1054   *DUDE RANCH* (1026)
1056   *DOWN ON THE FARM* - no date, but 1940's
1057   *PLAYHOUSE PAPER DOLLS* 1947 - (date in Lowe records)
1061   *HAYRIDE* (1056)
1061   *JALOPY PAPER DOLLS* (1045 Playtime)
1062   *PLAYGROUND* (1025 Turnabout)
1062   *BABY BUGGY* (1025 - 8 Ages of Judy)
1063   *BAB AND HER DOLL FURNITURE* (523)
1063   *JANIE AND HER DOLL* (523)
1063   *MARY AND HER TOYS* (523)
1063   *UNITED STATES SOLDIERS* 1942 - stand-ups
1064-1   *PRINCESS* (1242)
1064-2   *OUTDOOR GIRLS* (1246)
1064-3   *SALLY AND SUE* (1042 Pat)
1065   *MODEL TANKS CONSTRUCTION KIT* 1942 - stand-ups
1069   *MODEL AIRPLANES CONSTRUCTION KIT* 1942 - stand-ups
1072   *JANIE AND HER DOLL* (523)
1073   *BAB AND HER DOLL FURNITURE* (523)
1074   *MARY AND HER TOYS* (523)
1074   *DICK THE SAILOR* 1941, *TOM THE AVIATOR* 1941, *HARRY THE SOLDIER* 1941 - These are three separate books, but are tied together and sold as one book.

1076 *HAYRIDE* (1056)
1077 *JALOPY CUT-OUTS* (1045 Playtime)
1077 *LITTLE BEAR TO DRESS, LITTLE DOG TO DRESS, LITTLE PIG TO DRESS, LITTLE KITTEN TO DRESS.* These four books are tied together and sold as one book. No date, but they are pictured in the 1942 catalog and listed as new for 1942.
1078 *BABY BUGGY* (1025 - [8 Ages of Judy - dolls and clothes redrawn]
1079 *PLAYGROUND* (1025)-[Turnabout]
1081 *A BOX OF THREE DOLL BOOKS* (1021)-[Baby Show]
1083 *HERE COMES THE BRIDE* (1043)
1083 *NOVELTY BOX OF 10 DOLL BOOKS* (1021)-[Baby Show] for nine of the books and one book from #521 Little Cousins.
1085 *WILD WEST* (1026)-[Dude Ranch]
1085 *DUDE RANCH* (1026)
1085 *BIG ROUND UP* (1026)-[Dude Ranch]
1087 *THE BILT-UP BOOK OF MOTHER GOOSE* 1943 -Stand-up pages
1088 *THE BILT-UP BOOK OF LITTLE RED RIDING HOOD* 1943 - Stand-up pages
1089 *U.S. COMMANDOS* 1943 - stand-ups
1093 *UNITED STATES SAILORS PUNCH-OUT BOOK* 1942 -stand-ups
1226 *TWELVE CUT OUT DOLLS* 1944, (date is from Lowe records) - Box (1021)-[Baby Show]
1241 *CLOTHES MAKE A LADY* (1044)-[Mimi] doll and clothes redrawn
1242 *CINDERELLA STEPS OUT* 1948
1243 *FASHION CUT-OUTS WITH STURDIBILT DOLLS* (1046)-[Clothes Crazy]
1244 *LOTS OF STURDIBILT DOLLS* (1057)
1245 *STATUETTE DOLLS* (1048)-[Turnabouts]
1246 *FASHION PREVIEWS* 1949
1248 *TWELVE DOLLS* - Box (521A)
1248 *LET'S PLAY HOUSE* - no date, appeared in 1949 catalog
1249 *HANG UP YOUR DOLL CLOTHES* (958)-[Career Girls]
1250 *DOWN ON THE FARM* (1056)
1250 *HERE COMES THE BRIDE* (1043)
1250 *MODEL AIRPLANES* 1943 - stand-ups
1251 *MODEL TANKS* - 1943 - stand-ups
1251 *NEW TONI HAIR-DO DOLLS* 1951
1251 *SCHOOLMATES* (1049)-[Lollypop]
1252 *ROCKABYE BABIES* 1952 - (date in Lowe records)
1252 *SQUARE DANCE* (968)
1252 *COWBOY STAND-UPS* 1943
1253 *INDIAN STAND-UPS* 1943
1253 *PROM HOME PERMANENT* 1952
1253 *COEDS* (1253)-[Prom]
1254 *WE'RE THE JONES FAMILY* (2562)
1254 *THE BOBBSEY TWINS* 1952 - (date in Lowe records)
1254 *CAREER GIRLS* (958)
1254 *FARMYARD* 1943 - stand-ups
1255 *FAIRY PRINCESS* (1242)
1256 *BEAUTY QUEENS* - used dolls of Alice and Trixie from #2560 plus dolls from #2523.
1256 *ROSEMARY CLOONEY* 1953 - (date in Lowe records) (2585)
1257 *BABY PARADE* (1252)-[Rockabye]
1257 *THE BOBBSEY TWINS* (1254)
1258 *GLORIA'S MAKE UP* (2585)
1258 *SALLY THE STANDING DOLL* (1042)-[Pat]
1259 *FRITZI RITZ* (1251)-[Toni]
1260 *ANNIE THE SWEETHEART DOLL* 1956 (1283)
1262 *BABY DOLL* 1957 (2403)
1263 *LITTLE MAIDS DRESS SHOP* 1957 (2404)
1264 *TWO DOLLS* - Box (1045)-[Career Girls]
1264 *PRESSED BOARD DOLLS* (1025)-[8 Ages of Judy]
1265 *SERVICE KIT, LAND, SEA AND AIR* - stand-ups 1943
1266 *MODEL WAR PLANES* 1943 - stand-ups
1267 *MODEL TANK CONSTRUCTION KIT* 1943 - stand-ups
1280 *DIAPER DOLL* (1045)-[Wee Wee Baby]
1281 *FUN ON THE FARM* (1056)
1283 *CUDDLES AND RAGS* 1950 - (date in Lowe records)
1284 *TONI HAIR-DO CUT-OUT DOLLS* 1950
1286 *COWBOYS AND COWGIRLS* 1950 - (date in Lowe records)
1294 *THREE DOLLS MADE OF WOOD* - Box (521A)
1295 *TWENTY DOLLS* - Box (1021)-[Baby Show]
1319 *ENGINE 69* - coloring book with stand-ups on back cover.
1320 *FASHION PARADE* (1046)-[Clothes Crazy]
1320 *TWINKLE TWINS* (521 and 522)
1321 *THE TWELVE DOLL CUT-OUT BOOK* (521A and 1021 Baby Show)
1322 *HERE COMES THE BRIDE* (1043)
1322 *PLAYGROUND PAPER DOLLS* (1025)-[Turnabout]
1323 *PENNY GROWS UP* (1025)-[8 Ages of Judy]
1323 *PLAYMATES* (1025)-[Turnabout]
1323 *COLLEGE GIRLS* (1046)-[Clothes Crazy]
1324 *CUT-ME-OUT PAPER DOLLS* (523)-[Tom, Bab, Mary, Janie & Fred]
1324 *TWINKLE TWINS* (521 and 522)
1324 *THE FASHION MODELS* (1048)-[Turnabouts]
1325 *PLAYTIME PALS* (   )
1325 *DOLLS AT PLAY* (1025)-[Turnabout]
1325 *PLAYGROUND* (1025)-[Turnabout]
1325 *HAY RIDE* (1056)
1326 *HOLIDAY PAPER DOLLS* (521 and 522 Twinkle Twins)
1326 *JALOPY PAPER DOLLS* (1045)-[Playtime]
1326 *BIG BABY DOLL BOOK* (1045)-[Wee Wee Baby]

1327 *BABY BUGGY* (1025 - 8 Ages of Judy)
1327 *LOLLYPOP CROWD* (1049)
1327 *ANN AND BETTY* (521A) and (521 - Little Cousins)
1328 *PLAYGROUND* (1025 - Turnabout)
1328 *BROTHER AND SISTER DOLL BOOK* (521 and 522 - Twinkle Twins)
1329 *OUTDOOR GIRLS* (1246)
1329 *HOLIDAYS* (   )
1329 *SALLY AND SUE* (1042 Pat)
1329 *PRINCESS DOLLS* (   )
1331 *COSTUME PAPER DOLLS* (1842 - Ten cut-out dolls)
1331 *WEDDING PARTY* (1043)
1332 *JAMBOREE DOLL BOOK* (968)
1333 *CAMPUS QUEENS* (1046 - Clothes Crazy)
1334 *COWGIRLS DOLL BOOK* (1026 - Dude Ranch)
1335 *HOLLYWOOD DOLL BOOK* (958)
1335 *FRITZI RITZ* - Coloring book, Paper dolls but no outfits, dolls like #1259
1336 *MODELS DOLL BOOK* (1246)
1350 *FASHION PARADE DOLL BOOK* 1947 (1046 - Clothes Crazy)
1351 *THE FIRST SEVEN YEARS OF PENNY* (1025 - 8 Ages of Judy)
1352 *PLAYTIME PALS* (521 and 522 - Twinkle Twins)
1354 *THE OUTDOOR GIRLS* (1048 - Turnabouts)
1355 *BRIDE DOLL* (1043)
1356 *BLUE FEATHER AND SILVER CLOUD* (1044)
1357 *JUDY AND MARY* (1025 - Turnabout)
1358 *CUT-ME-OUT PAPER DOLLS* (523 - Tom, Bab, Janie, Fred and Mary)
1359 *BUSY DAYS* (521 and 522 - Twinkle Twins)
1360 *FARMYARD* (1056)
1361 *THE FIRST SEVEN YEARS OF PENNY* (1025 - 8 Ages of Judy)
1361 *LOTS OF DOLLS* (1057)
1362 *DUDE RANCH* (1026)
1363 *CAREER GIRLS* (   )
1366 *LOOK ALIKE DOLLS* (1284)
1367 *TV STAR TIME* 1955 (990)
1368 *TWINKLE TOTS* (1252 - Rockabye) and (1049 - Lollypop)
1369 *CUDDLES* (1283)
1370 *MY FAVORITE DOLL BOOK* (1254 - Bobbsey)
1371 *CAMPUS QUEEN* (1253 - Prom)
1372 *BIG 'N' LITTLE SISTER* (1284)
1372 *SCHOOLMATES* (1252 - Rockabye) and (1049 - Lollypop)
1373 *COEDS* (1253 - Prom)
1374 *DOTTY DIMPLE* (1283)
1374 *DANCE TEAM* (990)
1375 *SWEET SIXTEEN* (1253)-[Prom]
1375 *PARTY DOLLS* (990)
1376 *BIG SISTER* (1284)
1376 *SONNY AND SUE* (1049)-[Lollypop] and (1252)-[Rockabye]
1377 *PLAY DAYS PAPER DOLLS* (1254)-[Bobbsey]
1377 *LITTLE NEIGHBOR PAPER DOLLS* (1254)-[Bobbsey]
1378 *TEEN QUEENS* (1253)-[Prom]
1378 *VACATION TIME* (   )
1379 *ME AND MIMI* (1283)
1380 *SCHOOLMATES* (1049)-[Lollypop] and (1252)-[Rockabye]
1380 *TV STAR TIME* (990)
1381 *DRESS A LIKE* (1284)
1381 *CAMPUS QUEENS* (1253)-[Prom]
1382 *PLAY PALS* (1254)-[Bobbsey]
1382 *TWINKLE TOTS* (1252)-[Rockabye]
1383 *PARTY FASHIONS* (   )
1383 *CUDDLES* (1283)
1384 *MY FAVORITE DOLL BOOK* (1254)-[Bobbsey]
1384 *LOOK A LIKE* (1284)
1385 *BUSY DAYS* (521 and 522)-[Twinkle Twins]
1385 *TV STAR TIME* (990)
1385 *BROTHER AND SISTER* (522 and 521)-[Twinkle Twins]
1386 *COUNTRY COUSINS* (1056)
1386 *CAMPUS QUEENS* (   )
1386 *LOTS OF DOLLS* (1057)
1387 *SUNNY AND SUE* (1049)-[Lollypop] and (1252)-[Rockabye]
1387 *PROM DATE* (1046)-[Clothes Crazy]
1387 *THE OUTDOOR GIRLS* (1048)-[Turnabouts]
1388 *JALOPY* (1045)-[Playtime]
1388 *DRESS ALIKE* (1283)
1388 *SWING YOUR PARTNER* (968)
1389 *BIG SISTER IN PARIS* (958)-[Career Girls]
1389 *HERE COMES THE BRIDE* (1043)
1390 *FASHION PREVIEWS* (1246)
1390 *TV STYLE SHOW* (1246)
1391 *BOARDWALK PAPER DOLLS* (521 and 522)-[Twinkle Twins]
1391 *FUN ON THE FARM* (1056)
1392 *FUN ON THE FARM* (1056)
1392 *JUDY AND HER FRIENDS* (1046)-[Clothes Crazy]
1393 *PLAYHOUSE PAPER DOLLS* (1057)
1393 *FASHION PARADE* (1046)-[Clothes Crazy]
1394 *POLKA PARTY* (968)
1394 *BEACH PARTY* (521 and 522 - Twinkle Twins)
1395 *TELEVISION STARS* (1246)
1395 *CARNIVAL PAPER DOLLS* (1049 - Lollypop)
1396 *COWGIRLS, A REAL WESTERN DOLL BOOK* 1950 (1026 - Dude Ranch)
1396 *BIG SISTER* (958 - Career Girls)
1424 *ANN AND BETTY* (521A) and (521 - Little Cousins) Made for Best Maid Co.

1425-4 *PLAYROOM PAPER DOLLS*- Box - 5 books - contents similar to #8 and #L-24. This box set made up for the Best Maid Co.

1428 *THE TWELVE DOLL CUT-OUT BOOK* (521A) and (1021 Baby Show) Best Maid Co.

1442 *FOUR PLAYMATE CUT-OUT DOLLS* (1021 Baby Show) Best Maid Co.

1443 *BETTY BO PEEP* (1045 - Wee Wee Baby) Best Maid Co.

1513 *MOTHER AND DAUGHTER* (2562)

1514 *RUTH, JOAN AND WINNIE* (2404)

1515 *MR. AND MRS.* (2560)

1516 *JET AIRLINE STEWARDESS* (4913)

1517 *FASHION MODELS* (2488)

1518 *WENDY* (2915)

1531 *THE FIRST SEVEN YEARS OF PENNY* (1025 - 8 Ages of Judy)

1588 *WENDY* ( )

1589 *CELEBRITY AUTOGRAPH COLORING BOOK WITH PAPER DOLLS OF JANET LEIGH* 1958 (2405)

1801 *BABY DOLL* (2403)

1801A *LITTLE DRESSMAKER DOLL BOOK* - Betty Jane 1964 (1831 Lollipop Kids)

1801B *LITTLE DRESSMAKER DOLL BOOK* - Mary Ann 1964 (1829 Playmates)

1801C *LITTLE DRESSMAKER DOLL BOOK* - Sally Lou 1964 (1831 Lollipop Kids)

1802 *LITTLE SCHOOL MAIDS* (2404)

1802 *PLAYROOM PAPER DOLLS* - Box - Contents similar to #8 and #L-24 - 5 books.

1804 *PATTI PAGE* 1958 (2406)

1805 *JANET LEIGH* 1958 (2405)

1806 *ROSEMARY CLOONEY* 1959 (2585)

1807 *PATIENCE AND PRUDENCE* 1959 (2411)

1808 *THE THREE CHEERS* (1253 Prom)

1809 *HERE COMES THE BRIDE* (1043)

1810 *BOB CUMMINGS FASHION MODELS* (2407)

1810 *BONNIE DOLL* - Cut-out Book (2751) for the doll, and (2750 - Elizabeth) for the clothes.

1810 *BOY AND GIRL* - Teen Dolls (2407)

1811 *CUT-OUT BOOK* - Betsy Doll (3903)

1811 *CUTIE DOLL* cut-out book (1283)

1812 *CUT-OUT BOOK SUSAN DOLL* (3903)

1812 *HOLLYWOOD GLAMOUR* (2407)

1813 *CUT-OUT BOOK - SALLY DOLL* (3903)

1813 *THREE LITTLE MAIDS FROM SCHOOL ARE WE* (2404)

1814 *BRIDE DOLL BOOK* (2493)

1814 *CUT-OUT BOOK - CINDY DOLL* (3903)

1815 *GOING PLACES WITH MARY AND BILL* (2563)

1815 *NANCY AND HER DOLLS* (2750 Elizabeth) some clothes taken from 2751 Bonnie

1816 *BABY TO DRESS AND CARE FOR* (2749 - Baby Anne)

1817 *MIMI* (2422)

1818 *EMILY* (2423)

1819 *TRUDY* (2424)

1820 *VICKY* (2762)

1821 *JULIE* (2763 - Dolly Gets New Clothes)

1822 *CUT-OUT BOOK SUSAN* (3903)

1823 *CUT-OUT BOOK MARY* (1829 Playmates)

1824 *CUT-OUT BOOK SALLY* (3903)

1825 *CUT-OUT BOOK CINDY* (3903)

1825 *DOLL PARTY, SUE AND PENNY* (4207)

1826 *PUNCH-OUT AND DRESS BETSY AND BITSY* (1283)

1826 *CUT-OUT BOOK - BETSY DOLL* (3903)

1827 *TEEN AGE DOLLS* (1253 - Prom)

1827 *CUT-OUT BOOK - BETTY DOLL* (1831 Lollipop Kids)

1828 *MOTHER'S GIRL AND GRANDMOTHER'S DOLL* (2561)

1828 *DRESS DOLLY CUT-OUTS - LUCY* (1886)

1829 *DRESS DOLLY CUT-OUTS - JANIE* (1887)

1829 *PLAYMATES* 1961 (date in Lowe records)

1830 *DRESS DOLLY CUT-OUTS - PATTY* (1885)

1830 *FASHION MODELS* (2585)

1831 *PLAYHOUSE DOLLY "JO"* (2784 - Little Girls)

1831 *LOLLIPOP KIDS* 1961 (date in Lowe records)

1832 *PLAYHOUSE DOLLY "JILL"* (2784 - Little Girls)

1832 *LOTS OF DOLLS* 1961 (date in Lowe records) Dolls new, clothes from #1057 this book, #1832 is pictured

1833 *YOUNG COUPLE* (2407)

1833 *PLAYHOUSE DOLLY - JANE* (2784 - Little Girls)

1834 *BABY DOLL TO DRESS AND CARE FOR* (2749 - Baby Anne)

1834 *HONEYMOON DOLLS* (2493)

1835 *DOLL BOOK - SALLY AND SUE* (2785)

1835 *TWINS - JANE AND JILL* (4219)

1836 *DOLLS - MOLLY AND NINA* (1832 - Lots of Dolls)

1836 *MARY JANE - 10" Doll Punch and Dress* (1283)

1837 *BROTHER AND SISTER DOLLS* (1832 Lots of Dolls)

1837 *FASHION MODELS* - Laura and Joanne (2407)

1838 *PAPER DOLL PLAYMATES - TIM AND BARBARA* (1832 Lots of Dolls)

1838 *TEEN-AGE DOLLS* (2483)

1839 *DRESS-UP DOLL BOOK - SHERRY* (2785)

1839 *SISTERS* (2411)

1840 *MARGO TRAVELS TO FOREIGN COUNTRIES* (2714)

1840 *BABY SITTER* (1025 Turnabout and 1046 Clothes Crazy)

1841 *JILL - DOLL CUT-OUT BOOK* (2784 Little Girls)

1842 *JANE - DOLL CUT-OUT BOOK* (2784 Little Girls)

1842 *A BOX OF TEN CUT-OUT DOLLS* 1947 - (date in Lowe records) - John Martin's House trademark.

1842 *CUDDLY CUT-OUTS* (1252 Rockabye)

1843 *COVER GIRLS* (2407)

1843 *SANDRA - DOLL CUT-OUT BOOK* (2717 Grow Up)

1844 *DOLL TIME* (1284 and one small doll from #9041)

1844 *JANET - DOLL CUT-OUT BOOK* (2717 Grow Up)

1845 *SHIRLEY - DOLL CUT-OUT BOOK* (2717 Grow Up)

L1845 *TWO STORY DOLL HOUSE WITH PAPER DOLLS* from #1028 Playhouse (made for Sears)

1845 *TEEN-AGE SISTER DOLLS* (2411)

1846 *DORIS - DOLL CUT-OUT BOOK* (2721)

1846 *THE GIRLS NEXT DOOR* (2562)

1847 *PLAYHOUSE PAPER DOLLS* - Box of 6 paper dolls from the 1940's. The books varied as to titles available in stock.

1847 *SHERRY AND TERRY* - Doll Cut-out book (2722 Little Dolls)

1847 *SISTERS* (2411)

1848 *DOLL CUT-OUTS* 1971 ( )

1848 *SUE - Doll Cut-out Book* (2721)

1849 *SALLY - Doll Cut-out Book* (2785)

1849 *JUDY* ( )

1850 *JENNY AND NANCY* - Doll Cut-out Book (2723)

1851 *PEGGY AND TRUDY* - Doll Cut-out Book (2723)

1851 *ALL AMERICAN GIRLS* - Box - Combines dolls from four books - BRIDE DOLL #1043, THE TURNABOUTS #1048, CLOTHES CRAZY #1046 and DUDE RANCH #1026.

1852 *PLAYTIME PALS* - Large envelope contained assorted paper doll books from the late 1940's and early 1950's. Books varied as to titles available in stock.

1854 *CITY GIRL* 1963 (3903)

1855 *MAMMOTH BOX OF DOLLS AND DRESSES* - 29 Dolls from assorted books of the 1940's.

1855 *SCHOOLGIRL DOLL BOOK* 1963 (3903)

1856 *LOOK ALIKE* - Dress Alike 1963 Twins Doll Book (2404)

1857 *VACATION* 1963 (4207)

1858 *WHAT SHALL WE WEAR* 1963 (2404)

1860 *MOTHER AND DAUGHTER* 1963 (2411)

1861 *NURSE CUT-OUT DOLL* 1963 (4913)

1862 *MASQUERADE PARTY* 1963 (1832 Lots of Dolls)

1863 *DOLL BOOK* - Sherry and Jerry 1963 (2407)

1864 *SOCIETY DOLLS* 1963 (2488)

1865 *DOLLY GOES SHOPPING* 1964 (3921 Patti)

1866 *BABY DOLLS* (1252 Rockabye)

1867 *SCHOOLMATES* 1964 (2743 - Two Teens)

1868 *SISTER DOLLS* 1964 (2407)

1869 *DEBBIE AND DIANE* 1964 (2562)

1870 *NURSE CUT-OUT DOLL BOOK* 1964 (4913)

1871 *CITY GIRL* 1964 (3903)

1872 *SCHOOLGIRL* 1964 (3903)

1873 *ROSEMARY CLOONEY* - Box ( )

1873 *WHAT SHALL WE WEAR* (2404)

1874 *PENNY AND SUE* 1964 (4207)

1875 *SUSAN - CLOTHES FOR SCHOOL* (2743 - Two Teens)

1876 *PLAYMATES DOLL BOOK* 1964 - Mary and Bill (1056)

1877 *HELLO, PATTI* 1964 (3921)

1878 *HAIR-DO DOLL* 1964 (2743 - Two Teens)

1879 *SISTER DOLLS* 1964 (2411)

1880 *AIRLINE STEWARDESS* 1965 (4913)

1881 *PENNY GOES TO SCHOOL* 1965 (3903)

1882 *BABY DOLLS TO DRESS AND CARE FOR* 1965 (1252 -Rockabye)

1883 *DOLLY GOES SHOPPING* 1965 (3903)

1884 *SCHOOLGIRL* 1965 (2404)

1885 *PATTY - LITTLE DRESSMAKER DOLL BOOK* 1966

1886 *LUCY - LITTLE DRESSMAKER DOLL BOOK* 1966

1887 *JANIE - LITTLE DRESSMAKER DOLL BOOK* 1966

1888 *JANICE* ( )

1889 *SUSAN - HAIR-DO-DOLL* (2743 - Two Teens)

1890 *JACKIE - HAIR-DO-DOLL* (2743 - Two Teens)

1891 *BRIDESMAID DOLLS* (2562)

1892 *MARY* (1829 Playmates)

1893 *BETTY* (1831 Lollipop Kids)

1894 *SALLY* (1831 Lollipop Kids)

1902 *BOX OF DOLLS* ( )

1915 *SEW ON DOLLS* (2610)

1941 *LET'S PLAY HOUSE* - Box 6 books that may include any of the following books. #969 HOLLYWOOD DOLLS, #946 DOWN ON THE FARM, #1284 TONI, #945 BABY SITTER, #968 SQUARE DANCE, #1248 LET'S PLAY HOUSE, #1327 LOLLIPOP CROWD, #958 CAREER GIRLS and there may be others.

2103 *TOYTOWN MOTORAMA*, 1962 catalog stand-ups

2104 *COWBOYS AND INDIANS* 1961 stand-ups

2105 *PLAY HOUSEKEEPING* 1961 (1248)

2107 *MODEL VILLAGE*, 1962 catalog - stand-ups

2108 *PUNCH-OUT BAZAAR* - toys and stand-ups 1962 catalog

2109 *MASK-A-RADE* - Masks, 1962 catalog

2110 *SANTA'S BAND* 1962 - has two paper dolls and stand-ups

2110 *SANTA'S CHRISTMAS* 1968 (2110 Santa's Band)

2115 *PUNCH-OUT CIRCUS* 1963 stand-ups

2116 *TOYTOWN MOTORAMA* 1963 - stand-ups

2117 *PUNCH-OUT TOYS FOR GIRLS AND BOYS* 1963 stand-ups by John Dukes McKee

2118 *MY OWN ZOO* - stand-ups

2125 *PUNCH AND JUDY SHOW* 1967 and 1971 Puppets, stage and script

2127   *DOLL HOUSE FURNITURE* stand-ups
2128   *PLAY CITY* stand-ups
2129   *CIRCUS* stand-ups
2131   *FIRE ENGINE* stand-ups
2132   *FARM ANIMALS*, 1969 catalog, stand-ups
2134   *TOYLAND PUNCH-OUTS* 1970 paper toys
2138   *PUNCH-OUT FINGER PUPPETS* 1971
2139   *PLAYTOWN PUNCH-OUT* 1971 stand-ups
2212   *BUILD A CITY* 1962 Coloring book and punch-outs
2216   *MAIN ST.* 1963 - Coloring book and stand-ups
2217   *INDIANS* 1963 coloring book and stand-ups
2218   *REAL COWBOYS* 1963 coloring book and stand-ups
2240   *PUPPET PUNCH-OUT MARIONETTES*, 1969 catalog, coloring book and punch-outs
2241   *COWBOYS*, 1969 catalog, coloring book and stand-ups
2242   *INDIANS*, 1969 catalog, coloring book and stand-ups
2360   *HIS PEEK-A-BOOK* 1961 - story book with costume on each page (2563)
2361   *HER PEEK-A-BOOK* 1961 - story book with costume on each page (2563)
2403   *BABY DOLL* 1957
2404   *THREE LITTLE MAIDS FROM SCHOOL ARE WE* 1957
2405   *JANET LEIGH* 1957
2406   *PATTI PAGE* 1957
2407   *BOB CUMMINGS FASHION MODELS* 1957
2408   *THE THREE CHEERS* 1957 (1253 Prom)
2411   *PATIENCE AND PRUDENCE* 1957
2419   There are over 30 different packets with this number. Each consists of paper doll books with other numbers mentioned elsewhere in this list. Usually two books are in each packet but not always.
2420   *SIX CUT-OUTS AND LOVELY CLOTHES* (1832 Lots of Dolls)
2421-A   *ALIVE-LIKE BABY DOLL* (2749 Baby Anne)
2421-B   *ALIVE-LIKE DOLLY* (2751 Bonnie)
2421-C   *ALIVE-LIKE DOLLY* (2750 Elizabeth)
2422   *MIMI - DOLL KEEPSAKE* 1964
2423   *EMILY - DOLL KEEPSAKE* 1964
2424   *TRUDY - DOLL KEEPSAKE* 1964
2426   *FASHION DESIGNER - PATTY* (1885)
2426   *FASHION DESIGNER - LUCY* (1886)
2426   *FASHION DESIGNER - JANIE* (1887)
2427   *LITTLE MISS PAINT BY NUMBERS* - Dress Designer Set (2574 Betsy)
2431E   *SIX CUT-OUT PAPER DOLLS* (1832 Lots of Dolls)
2438-A   *A LITTLE MISS SEW AND SEW* - Clothes Lace-On (1283)
2438-B   *LITTLE MISS SEW AND SEW* - Clothes Lace-On (1283)
2438-C   *LITTLE MISS SEW AND SEW* - Clothes Lace-On (1283)
2480   *ROSEMARY CLOONEY* 1958 (2585)
2481   *JANET LEIGH - HOLLYWOOD GLAMOUR* 1958 (2405)
2482   *SWEETIE PIE* 1958 (1283)
2483   *JUNIOR MISSES* 1958
2484   *VACATION ALBUM* 1958 (2407)
2485   *PENNY'S PARTY* 1958 (4207)
2486   *MILLION DOLLAR DOLLS* 1958 (2407)
2487   *ROSEMARY CLOONEY* 1958 (2585)
2488   *PATTI PAGE* 1958
2489   *ROSEMARY CLOONEY* 1958 (   )
2490   *BROTHER AND SISTER* 1959 (2563)
2491   *SCHOOL DAYS* 1959 (2404)
2492   *SWEETEST BABY* 1959 (2403)
2493   *BRIDE AND GROOM* 1959
2494   *SISTERS* 1959 (2411)
2502   *CHRISTMAS FUN BOOK* 1974 - coloring book and paper toys
2508   *PAM AND HER PRAM* 1956 - Paper doll and coloring book. Dolls on the back cover are from #1284 and the doll inside is from #2574 (Betsy).
2515   *GLORIA'S MAKE-UP PAPER DOLL* (2585)
2522   *PAPER PLAYMATES, JAN AND JIMMY* 1955 (2563)
2523   *KAY AND KIM WITH CLOTHES TO TRIM* 1956
2528   *ANNIE THE ACTION DOLL* 1954 (1283)
2530   *LITTLE MISS MUFFET* (1283)
2531   *BETSY AND BOB* (1286)
2532   *PATIENCE AND PRUDENCE* (2411)
2539   *CHILDREN'S PARTY PACK* - Contains three assorted paper doll books
2556   *SEWING CARD BOOK WITH SEW ON CLOTHES* 1953 - Five dolls taken from three different books, (#1045 *PLAYTIME PALS*, #1284 *TONI* and #1252 *ROCKABYE*)
2559   *DOTTY DIMPLE* (1283)
2560   *THE HONEYMOONERS* 1956
2561   *GOLDILOCKS* 1955
2562   *HERE COMES THE BRIDE* 1955
2563   *HIS AND HERS* - The Guest Towel Dolls 1955
2564   *TEEN QUEENS* 1955 (1253 Prom)
2565   *SCHOOLMATES* (1049 Lollypop)
2566   *ROSEMARY CLOONEY* 1954 (2585)
2567   *KIT AND KAPOODLE* 1954 (4267 and 4268)
2568   *BETTY BUTTERCUP* (1283)
2569   *ROSEMARY CLOONEY* 1956
2572   *TANKS AND PLANES* 1943 - stand-ups
2573   *SOLDIERS AND SAILORS* 1943 - stand-ups
2574   *DOLL HOUSE FURNITURE* 1943 - stand-ups
2574   *PAINT BETSY'S SUNDAY BEST* 1955 - date in Lowe records. This is a Paint book, doll and clothes to be painted with the brush and paints included.
2575   *BARNYARD ANIMALS* 1943 - stand-ups
2576   *TEN DOLLS* - Box - 1947 catalog (   )

2582   *ANNIE THE ACTION DOLL* 1954 (1283)
2585   *GLORIA'S MAKE-UP* 1952 - date in Lowe records. This was the original of the Rosemary Clooney paper dolls. The doll was redrawn and six of the eight pages of clothes used in the Gloria Book were retained in the Rosemary Clooney books.
2589   *FIVE WOOD DOLLS* - Box (1025)-[Judy]
2591   *SIX PRESSBOARD DOLLS* 1942 - Box (1021)-[Baby Show]
2593   *HIGH CHAIR TO HIGH SCHOOL* - cut-out dolls - Box 1952 catalog. Contained five paper doll books of assorted titles from Lowe stock.
2595   *ROSEMARY CLOONEY PAPER DOLL AND COLORING BOOK* 1956 (2585)
2596   *TWO IN ONE COLOR AND CUT-OUT BOOK* - Penny and Sue (4207)
2610   *SALLY'S DRESS A DOLL STORYBOOK* 1952 - date in Lowe records. Some of these dolls were produced with children's hankerchiefs one for each day of the week included inside the book.
2701   *ANNIE THE STATUETTE DOLL* 1956 (1283)
2702   *PARTY DOLLS* 1956 (990)
2703   *FASHION MODELS* 1956 (1048-[The Turnabouts]
2704   *BETSY AND BOB* (1286)
2705   *KIT AND KAPOODLE* 1956 (4267 and 4268)
2706   *DOLLY AND ME* 1956 (1284)
2707   *SQUARE DANCE* 1957 (968)
2708   *LET'S PLAY HOUSE* 1957 (1248)
2709   *FAIRY PRINCESS* 1957 (1242)
2709   *DOLLIES GO SHOPPING* (   )
2710   *DOLLS AND DRESSES* - Patty and Jan 1971 (1885 and 1887)
2710   *TEEN QUEENS* 1957 (1253)-[Prom]
2711   *DOTTY DIMPLE* 1957 (1283)
2711   *DOLLS AND CLOTHES* 1971 (2422 and 2423)
2712   *TWO TEENS* 1971 (2743)
2713   *ROSEMARY CLOONEY* 1957 (2585)
2713   *MOPSY AND POPSY* 1971
2714   *DOLLIES GO 'ROUND THE WORLD* 1971
2715   *DRESS THE DOLLIES* - Penny and Sue 1971 (4207)
2716   *COUNTRY AND WESTERN* 1971 (968)
2717   *SEW ON DOLL AND CLOTHES* - Little Miss Sew and Sew (1283)
2717   *WHEN WE GROW UP* 1971
2718   *HERE COMES THE BRIDE* 1971
2719   *MOTHER AND DAUGHTER* 1971 (2411)
2719   *I'M A BIG CRY BABY* - doll has noise maker (2403)
2720   *DRESS ANNABELLE* 1972
2721   *DOLL FRIENDS* 1972
2722   *LITTLE DOLLS* 1972
2722   10" statuette doll with 5 dresses to sew on with yarn (   )
2723   *A HOUSE FULL OF DOLLS AND CLOTHES* 1972
2724   *NOW AND THEN PAPER DOLLS* 1973
2725   *THE HAPPY FAMILY* 1973
2728   *DRESS UP DOLLS* 1969 (2411)
2730   *POLLY PAL* (3730)
2730   *POLLY AND HER DOLLY* 1971 (9118)
2731   *ROSEMARY CLOONEY* 1958 (2585)
2731   *SCHOOLMATES* (1049)-[Lollypop]
2732   *BOB CUMMINGS FASHION MODELS* 1958 (2407)
2732   *FASHION MODELS* (1251)-[Toni]
2733   *JANET LEIGH* 1958 (2405)
2733   *CAREER GIRLS* (958)
2734   *CINDERELLA* 1960 (1242)
2734   *PATTI PAGE* 1958 (2406)
2735   *GLAMOUROUS HIGH FASHION* 1958 (2407)
2735   *AFTER SCHOOL PARTY* - Bandstand (2483)
2736   *DUET DOLLS*, featuring Patience and Prudence 1958 (2411)
2736   *HIS AND HERS* - The Guest Towel Dolls (2563)
2737   *HERE COMES THE BRIDE* 1962 (2493)
2738   *SCHOOLGIRLS* 1962 (2404)
2738   *CUDDLES AND RAGS* (1283)
2739   *PATTI PAGE* 1959 (2406)
2739   *AIRLINE STEWARDESS* 1962 (4913)
2740   *DR. KILDARE AND NURSE SUSAN* 1962 - The dolls for Nurse Susan come from #4913 Airline Stewardess with some of their clothes. Dolls are redrawn. The doll for Dr. Kildare comes from #2407 - Bob Cummings and some of his clothes. Doll is redrawn. There are two different front covers for this book #2740. One has a blue background and is signed by Pollard. The other has a red background, is not signed.
2740   *TEENS* 1959 (2483)
2741   *CHEERLEADERS* 1962 (2483)
2741   *PARTY DOLLS* 1959 (4207)
2742   *TWINKLES* 1963
2742   *SCHOOL CHILDREN* 1963 (1832)-[Lots of Dolls]
2742   *AIRLINE STEWARDESS* 1959 (4913)
2743   *MIMI* 1966 New clothes, doll from #3905
2743   *CELEBRITY FASHION SHOW* (2407)
2743   *TWO TEENS* 1963
2744   *BABY SISTER* 1966 (2403)
2744   *LITTLE MISS MUFFET* 1959 (1283)
2745   *DRESS UP DOLLS* 1963 (2560)
2745   *MY BIG DOLLY* 1966 (5908)
2745   *CUDDLES* (   )
2748   *CELEBRITY FASHION SHOW* 1959 (   )
2748   *SATURDAY NIGHT BARN DANCE* (968)
2749   *DOLLS AND THEIR DOLLIES* 1961 (1284)
2749   *BABY ANNE SMILES AND CRIES* 1964

2750 *ALIVE LIKE DOLL - ELIZABETH* 1963
2750 *COLLEGE GIRLS* ( )
2750 *ROYAL PRINCESS* 1961 (2406 and 2488)
2751 *BONNIE - ALIVE LIKE DOLLY* 1963
2751 *BIG DOLL BETTY* 1960 (date in Lowe records)
2752 *SCHOOL TIME* 1964 (1832)-[Lots of Dolls]
2752 *LOOK ALIKE TWINS* (2904)
2753 *DOLLIES GO SHOPPING* copyright 1964 and 1969 (2422 and 2423)
2753 *SIX SCHOOL GIRL DOLLS* 1961 (2404)
2754 *THE JONES FAMILY* 1961 (2562)
2754 *BETTY BUTTERCUP* 1964 (1283)
2754 *THE BOBBSEY TWINS* (1254)
2755 *SALLY AND JANE* 1964 (2743)-[Two Teens]
2755 *BRIDE AND GROOM* 1961 (2493)
2756 *SWEETIE PIE* ( )
2756 *LIFE LIKE ANIMATED FACES DOLL* 1964 (2751)-[Bonnie]
2756 *ROCK-A-BYE BABIES* (1252)
2757 *MOLLY DOLLY* 1965 (5908)
2757 *LITTLE CALENDAR GIRL* - Doll comes from #2906, clothes from #2751 -Betty
2757 *JANET LEIGH* 1957 (2405)
2758 *PENNY'S PARTY* 1965 (4207)
2758 *PATTI PAGE* 1957 (2406)
2758 *LITTLE BALLERINA* 1961 (2915)
2759 *FIFTH AVENUE DOLL BOOK* 1961 (2405)
2759 *PATTI ALIVE-LIKE DOLL BOOK* 1965 (3921)
2759 *REAL NURSE* (958)-[Career Girls]
2760 *DOTTY DOLL BOOK* 1968 - doll is redrawn, clothes from #2743 Mimi -This book is pictured as it has reprints of its own.
2760 *THREE DOLLS*, Clothes for School, Parties, Play and Proms 1961 (1046 Clothes Crazy)
2761 *DOLLIES GO TO SCHOOL* ( )
2761 *BABY DOLL* 1957 (2403)
2761 *SISTER DOLLS* 1964 also dated 1966 (2411)
2761 *MY VERY OWN BABY DOLL* 1967 (2749)-[Baby Anne]
2762 *THREE YOUNG LADIES* 1964 (2404)
2762 *GIRLS DEPARTMENT* (2404)
2762 *LITTLE MAIDS DRESS SHOP* 1957 (2404)
2762 *VICKY* 1967 - This book is pictured even though a reprint of #2751 Bonnie, as it has reprints of its own.
2763 *DOLLY GETS LOTS OF NEW CLOTHES* 1967 (2750)-[Elizabeth] This book #2763 is pictured.
2763 *HOOTENANNY* - Country and Western 1964 (968)
2764 *PIXIE DOLL AND PUP* 1968
2764 *DRESS UP ANIMALS* (4267 and 4268)
2764 *ARCHIES GIRLS* 1964 (2483)
2765 *WESTERN COWGIRL AND COWBOY* (1286)
2765 *WE'RE THE JONES FAMILY* 1958 (2562)
2766 *FRONT AND BACK DOLLS AND DRESSES* 1964
2766 *CUT-OUT DOLLS WESTERN STYLE CLOTHES* 1958 (968)
2766 *HAIR-DOS* 1960 (2493)
2767 *DIMPLES* 1958 - Best Dressed Baby Doll in Town (2403)
2767 *GOLDILOCKS* 1964 (2561)
2768 *TINA AND HER FRIENDS* 1960 (1253)-[Prom]
2768 *CAMPUS QUEENS* 1958 (1253)-[Prom]
2768 *DR. KILDARE* - Nurse dolls from #4913 and Dr. from #2407 (dolls redrawn)
2768 *HELLO DOLLIES* 1964 (2424 for large doll and 9118 for small doll)
2769 *SCHOOLMATES* 1960 (1056)
2769 *CAREER GIRLS* (958)
2769 *DOLLIES GO TO SCHOOL* 1971 (2404)
2770 *HOLIDAY CRUISE* 1965 (2483)
2770 *CINDERELLA* 1958 (1242)
2771 *SUZY* 1966 (5901)
2771 *HOLLYWOOD GLAMOUR* - Janet Leigh 1966 (2405)
2772 *AFTER SCHOOL PARTY* - Bandstand 1958 (2483)
2772 *HELLO, PATTI* 1967 (3921)
2773 *SCHOOLMATES* 1958 (2404)
2773 *SCHOOLMATES* 1967 (2743)-[Two Teens]
2774 *ROSEMARY CLOONEY* 1958 (2569)
2774 *TWINKLES* 1967 (2563)
2775 *POLLY AND HER DOLLY* 1968 (9118)
2775 *BOY MEETS GIRL* - Jerry and Sherry 1958 (2407)
2775 *SALLY AND JANE* 1964 ( )
2776 *MOLLY DOLLY* 1968 (5908)
2776 *FABULOUS HIGH FASHION MODELS* 1958 (2407)
2777 *BETTY DOLL* 1968 (2563) - dolls and clothes redrawn
2778 *DRESS UP DOLLS* 1969 (2411)
2779 *DOLLS AND DRESSES* 1969 (1885, 1886, 1887)
2780 *DOLLIES TRY ON NEW CLOTHES* 1969 (2762 Vicky and 2763 Dolly)
2781 *GIRLS AND BOYS* - dated 1969 and 1973 (1832 Lots of Dolls)
2782 *DOLLIES FASHION SHOW* 1969 (2750 Elizabeth) and (2751 Bonnie)
2782 *GIRLS DEPARTMENT* (2404)
2783 *THREE MODELS AND HAIR-DOS* (2493)
2783 *DOLLTIME CUT-OUT BOOK* 1969 (1829 Playmates and 1831 Lollipop Kids)
2784 *LITTLE GIRLS* 1969
2784 *HAIR-DO DOLLS* (2411)
2785 *BRENDA LEE* 1961 - (2407) Dolls redrawn, some new clothes added.
2785 *GLORIA'S MAKE-UP* (2585)

2785 *SALLY, SUE AND SHERRY* 1969
2786 *DR. KILDARE* 1962 - dolls of Nurse from #4913 and the doll of Dr. from #2407 (dolls are redrawn)
2786 *BABY SUE* 1969 (2403)
2787 *FAIRY TALE PRINCESS* 1962 (1242)
2787 *LITTLE MISS MUFFET* 1969 (1283)
2789 *FASHION MODELS* (1251 Toni)
2791 *DOWN ON THE FARM* ( )
2792 *GIRL FRIENDS* (2411)
2793 *HERE COMES THE BRIDE* (2493)
2794 *STORYBOOK DOLLS* 1959 (2563)
2795 *GOLDILOCKS* 1959 (2561)
2796 *BETTY BUTTERCUP* (1283)
2797 *BUSY TEENS* 1959 (2483)
2802 *STATUETTE DOLLS* (1049 Lollypop Crowd)
2886 *BABY SUE* 1969 (2403)
2903 *11" DOLL WITH BUTTON-ON CLOTHES* (2563)
2904 *SHERRY ANN'S SEW ON CLOTHES* 1960
2906 *BETSY DRESS A DOLL* 1960
2915 *WENDY DRESS A DOLL* 1959 - new doll, clothes same as #2610
2917 *FOUR STATUETTE DOLLS* - (2407 and 4207)
2930 *TWO SISTER DOLLS* (2411)
2930-1 *HERE COMES THE BRIDE* 1962 (2493)
2930-2 *SCHOOLMATES* 1962 (2404)
2930-3 *GIRL FRIENDS* 1962 (2411)
2930-4 *DIMPLES* - Best Dressed Baby Doll In Town 1962 (2403)
2932 *LOOK I'M ALIVE-LIKE* (3903)
2990 *SALLY'S SEW ON CLOTHES* (2610)
2992 *MAKE BELIEVE BEAUTY PARLOR* 1959 - Wigs to punch-out and put on life size head.
3362 *MASQUERADE PARTY* - Peek-a-Book (4299)
3363 *SHERLOCK BONES* - Peek-a-Book (4263)
3364 *TREASURE LAND* - Peek-a-Book (4298)
3365 *DOLLY GOES AROUND THE WORLD* - Peek-a-Book (4264)
3366 *SHADOW* - Peek-a-Book (4267)
3367 *KITTY* - Peek-a-Book (4268)
3368 *ALFIE* - Peek-a-Book (4344)
3379 *HIS* - Peek-a-Book (2563)
3380 *HER* - Peek-a-Book (2563)
3711 *LITTLE DOLLS* 1974 (2722)
3711 *FOUR PUSH-OUT DOLLS TO DRESS* 1976 (2722 Little Dolls)
3712 *MS. DOLLS* 1976 (2717 - Grow Up)
3712 *WHEN WE GROW UP* 1974 (2717)
3713 *DOLL PUSH-OUTS* 1974 (2721)
3714 *DOLL PUSH-OUTS* 1974 (2785 - Sally, Sue and Sherry)
3715 *NOW AND THEN* 1976 (2724)
3716 *BABY SISTER* 1974 (2403)
3717 *MOPSY AND POPSY* - dated 1974 and 1976 (2713)
3718 *GOLDILOCKS AND THE THREE BEARS* 1975 (2561)
3719 *MY VERY OWN BABY DOLL* 1974 (2749 - Baby Anne)
3720 *DOLLIES GO ROUND THE WORLD* 1974 (2714)
3721 *TWO TEENS* 1974 (2743)
3722 *LITTLE GIRLS* 1974 (2784)
3723 *HERE COMES THE BRIDE* 1975 (2718)
3724 *A HOUSE FULL OF DOLLS AND CLOTHES* 1975 (2723)
3725 *THE HAPPY FAMILY* 1973 (2725)
3726 *SCHOOL CHILDREN* 1975 (1832 - Lots of Dolls)
3727 *JEANNIE AND GENE* published in 1975 and 1976
3730 *POLLY PAL* 1976.
3851 *PUNCH-OUT MERRY-GO-ROUND* 1974 - stand-ups
3855 *DOLLHOUSE FURNITURE* 1967 Stand-ups
3856 *PUNCH-OUT AND FOLD - PLAY CITY* - Downtown 1967 stand-ups
3903 *MARY ANN* - animated face 1960 - (date in Lowe records)
3903 *SALLY ANN* - animated face 1960 - (date in Lowe records)
3903 *BETTY ANN* - animated face 1960 - (date in Lowe records)
3905 *MIMI FROM PAREE* 1960
3906 *BETSY DOLL AND CLOTHES* (2906)
3909A - *STAND-UP DOLL-SEW ON* (2760 - Dotty)
3909B - *STAND-UP DOLL-SEW ON* (2563)
3909C - *STAND-UP DOLL-SEW ON* (2563)
3909D - *STAND-UP DOLL-SEW ON* (2720)
3909E - *STAND-UP DOLL-SEW ON* (2720)
3909F - *STAND-UP DOLL-SEW ON* (2720)
3910 *DRESS MAKER SET* - Three different sets with the same number. Each comes with a doll, clothes, paints, brush and small scissors. Two dolls are from #1831 LOLLIPOP KIDS, one doll from #1829 PLAYMATES.
3911 *MAKE DOLLY'S CLOTHES* - Fashion Designer Set - Janie (1887)
3912 *MY BIG DOLLY TO DRESS AND READ TO* (5908 Molly Dolly)
3920 *TRIXIE* 1961 (2403)
3921 *PLAYMATES - DOLL HOUSE DOLLIES* 1966 (1885, 1886, 1887)
3921 *PATTI DOLL BOOK* 1961 - ALIVE LIKE FACE. Doll new, clothes from #3903. This book #3921 is pictured as it has reprints of its own.
3922 *DOLL HOUSE DOLLIES* 1966 (1829 Playmates and 1831 Lollipop Kids)
3923 *SCHOOLDAYS* - Doll House Dollies 1966 (1832 Lots of Dolls)
3924 *SISTERS* - Doll House Dollies 1966 (2411)
3925 *DOLL HOUSE BABIES* 1966 (1252 Rockabye)
3926 *GOLDILOCKS* - Doll House Dollies 1966 (2561)
3937 *EYES ON MARGIE* - Dress A Doll Storybook (2751 Betty)
3938 *EYES ON NANCY* - Dress A Doll Storybook (2904)
3941 *MY DOLLY TWINKLE* (5908)

3942 *MY DOLLY KISSES* (5908)
3944 *NANCY DRESS A DOLL STORYBOOK* 1964 - doll from #9045, clothes from #2904
3945 *WENDY* - Storybook Doll 1964 - Doll from #9045, clothes from #2915
3946 *BETSY* - Storybook Doll 1964 - Doll from #9118, clothes from #2906
3947 *CINDY* - Storybook Doll 1964 - all original
3967 *LITTLE SISTER* 1969 (   )
3972 *FAIRGROUND* (1049 Lollypop)
4008 *MY FIRST PAPER DOLL BOOK* - Bonnie Book (1057)
4009 *BYE BABY BUNTING* 1954 - Bonnie Book type of book (4219)
4171 *GABBY HAYES* 1954 - Jack-in-the-Book - Bonnie Book
4206 *ME AND MIMI* 1952, also 1953 - Bonnie Book (1283)
4207 *PENNY'S PARTY* 1952 - Bonnie book
4208 *MY VERY FIRST PAPER DOLL BOOK* - Bonnie Book 1952 (1057)
4214 *PENNY AND SUE* 1953 - Bonnie Book (4207)
4219 *BYE BABY BUNTING* 1952, also 1953 - Bonnie Book type of book
4220A *POLLY DOLLY* 1969 (9118)
4220B *MOLLY DOLLY* 1969 (2764 Pixie)
4220C *BABY DOLL* 1969 (2403)
4238 *DOLLY TAKES A TRIP* 1957 - Bonnie Book (4283)
4263 *SHERLOCK BONES* 1955 - Bonnie Book
4264 *DOLLY GOES ROUND THE WORLD* 1955 - Bonnie Book
4265 *BILLY BOY* 1953, also 1955 - Jack-in-the-Book. Bonnie Book
4266 *BETTY PLAYS LADY* 1953 Jack-in-the-Book. Bonnie Book
4267 *POPSY* 1953 - Jack-in-the-Book. Bonnie Book
4268 *TRINKET* 1953 - Jack-in-the-Book. Bonnie Book
4270 *MIMI* 1953 - Bonnie Book (1283)
4281 *CIRCUS TIME* 1952 - Jack-in-the-Book. Bonnie Book
4282 *LITTLE SUGAR BEAR* 1952 - Jack-in-the-Book. Bonnie Book
4283 *DOLLY TAKES A TRIP* 1952 - Jack-in-the-Book. Bonnie Book
4284 *COOKIE THE RABBIT* 1952 - Jack-in-the-Book. Bonnie Book
4298 *JUNGLETOWN JAMBOREE* 1955 - Bonnie Book
4299 *MASQUERADE PARTY* 1955 - Bonnie Book
4308 *MY FAVORITE DOLL BOOK* 1954 Bonnie Book (1057)
4343 *CAPTAIN BIG BILL* 1956 - Jack-in-the-Book. Bonnie Book
4344 *ALFIE* 1956 - Jack-in-the-Book. Bonnie Book
4345 *TIMMY* 1956 - Jack-in-the-Book. Bonnie Book
4420 *PENNY'S PARTY* - Bonnie Book (4207)
4501 *TALL TALES* 1963 - Jack-in-the-Book. Bonnie Book
4501 *I'M AMY - I'M JILL* 1974 (2760)
4502 *CIRCUS* 1964 - Jack-in-the-Book Story, listed in 1964 Lowe catalog
4502 *I'M MIMI - I'M JUDY* 1974 (2720)
4503 *BIG BILL* 1964 - Jack-in-the-Book Story, listed in 1964 Lowe catalog
4503 *I'M GINNY - I'M LOLLY* 1974 (2563) dolls and clothes redrawn
4504 *I'M TRUDY - I'M KATIE* 1974 (1283)
4505 *SCHOOL CHILDREN* 1975 also 1978 (1832 Lots of Dolls)
4506 *SALLY AND JANE* 1964, also 1978 (2743 Two Teens)
4507 *A HOUSE FULL OF DOLLS* 1975 (2723)
4508 *MS. DOLLS* 1976 (2717 Grow Up)
4509 *NOW AND THEN* 1976 (2724)
4509-D *STURDY STAND-UP DOLLY* (lace-on) (2720)
4509-E *STURDY STAND-UP DOLLY* (lace-on) (2720)
4509-F *STURDY STAND-UP DOLLY* (lace-on) (2720)
4510 *JEANNIE AND JEAN* 1976 (3727)
4531 *HERE COMES THE BRIDE* 1975 (2718)
4532 *THE HAPPY FAMILY* 1973 (2725)
4533 *DOLLIES GO ROUND THE WORLD* (2714)
4534 *POLLY PAL* (3730)
4535 *GOLDILOCKS AND THE THREE BEARS* 1975 (2561)
4536 *LITTLE GIRLS* 1974 (2784)
4701 *LITTLE BOY MEETS LITTLE GIRL* 1957 - Bonnie book (1254)
4704 *ADVENTURES OF TV TIM* 1957 - Bonnie Book - New doll, rest of book like - #4171
4730 *BYE BABY BUNTING* 1957 - Bonnie Book type of book (4219)
4731 *ME AND MIMI* - Bonnie Book (1283)
4732 *MY VERY FIRST PAPER DOLL* - Bonnie Book (1057)
4851 *FIRE DEPARTMENT* 1975 - stand-ups
4852 *ZOO STAND-UP ANIMALS* 1975 - stand-ups
4853 *PUNCH-OUT AND PLAY TOYS FOR BOYS* 1975 - paper toys
4854 *PUNCH AND JUDY* 1975 - puppets
4586 *FINGER PUPPETS* 1975 - puppets
4858 *FARM ANIMALS* 1976 - stand-ups
4859 *MASK-A-RADE* Punch-outs - Masks
4881 *MOLLY DOLLY* 1969 (5908)
4882 *GOLDILOCKS AND THE THREE BEARS* 1969 (2561)
4883 *PATTI, PINK - PERT AND PETITE* 1969 (3921)
4884 *SUZY* 1969 (5901)
4886 *SCHOOL BOY DOLL* 1963 (9301)
4887 *SCHOOL GIRL DOLL* 1963 (9302)
4909-D *STAND-UP DOLLY* 1972 - Lace-on clothes (2720)
4909-E *STAND-UP DOLLY* 1972 - Lace-on clothes (2720)
4909-F *STAND-UP DOLLY* 1972 - Lace-on clothes (2720)
4913 *AIRLINE STEWARDESS* 1957
4930-A *WENDY* 1970 Doll from #9045, clothes from #2915
4930-B *NANCY* 1970 Doll from #9045, clothes from #2904
4930-C *CINDY* 1970 (3947)
5751 *GIANT FUN PACK* in 1966 catalog. Contents appear to be same as #9211

5752 *WORLD WIDE ACTIVITY PACK* - in 1966 catalog. Appears to be same as #9212
5753 *BETSY DOLL PACK* (9118)
5754 *DOLL BABY PACK* (2403)
5755 *DRESSMAKER SET* (2750 Elizabeth) and (2751 Bonnie)
5756 *HELLO DOLLIES DOLL PACK* (3947) and (1832 Lots of Dolls)
5759 *KEEPSAKE DOLLS READ AND DRESS* - Four different packets with this same number. Each contained one of the Dress-a-doll Storybooks, either #3944, #3945, #3946 or #3947 plus two small paper doll books which varied.
5801 *PATTI PAGE* 1958 (2406) Stauette Dolls in a folder shaped like a purse. Included in the purse is a make-up kit, make-up chart and appointment book.
5842 *PLANES - MINIATURE MODELS* 1965 - stand-ups
5844 *MOTHER GOOSE PUNCH-OUT ACTIVITY* 1961 -stand-ups
5846 *CIRCUS PUNCH-OUT* stand-ups 1970
5901 *SUZY* - Alive Like Face Doll 1961
5908 *MOLLY DOLLY* 1962 - new doll, clothes partly new, some from #3905
5908 *MY DOLLY TWINKLE* 1962 (5908 Molly Dolly)
5908 *MY DOLLY KISSES* 1963 (5908 Molly Dolly)
5909 *DOLLIES GO SHOPPING* 1962 (3903)
5909 *ALIVE-LIKE DOLLS* 1963 (3903)
5909-G *LACE-ON CLOTHES DOLLY* 1975 (2760 Dotty)
5909-H *LACE-ON CLOTHES DOLLY* 1975 (2760 Dotty)
5905-I *LACE-ON CLOTHES DOLLY* 1975 (2563)
5909-J *LACE-ON CLOTHES DOLLY* 1975 (2563)
5911-A *DOLL DRESSMAKER* 1972 Janie (1887)
5911-B *DOLL DRESSMAKER* 1972 Patty (1885)
5911-C *DOLL DRESSMAKER* 1972 Lucy (1886)
5961 *LITTLE SISTER* 1969 (9041)
5962 *BIG SISTER JILL* 1969 (9302)
6901 *FAIRY PRINCESS DOLL* with animated face 1960 (1242)
6907 *HELLO DOLLIES* (3903)
6918 *BETSY DOLL* 1969 (9118)
6919 *BABY DOLL* 1969 (2403)
6920 *MAKE DOLLIES CLOTHES* - Paint by number (2750 Elizabeth) and (2751 Bonnie)
7502 *DOLL HOUSE* - Box with doll house and stand-up furniture 1943
8045 *HELLO DOLLIES* 1973 - lace-on costumes (2720)
8730 *KEEPSAKE DOLLY* - Mopsy and Popsy (2713)
8731 *KEEPSAKE DOLLY* - Jill and Jane (2784 Little Girls)
8732 *DRESSMAKER DOLL* (1829 Playmates and 1831 Lollipop Kids)
8733 *DOTTY* (2760)
8902 *LACE AND DRESS PUPPY* 1975
8903 *LACE AND DRESS KITTY* 1975
9000 *ROSEMARY CLOONEY* (2585) portfolio with paper dolls and coloring book
9041 *PEGGY AND PETER*, The Big, Big, Doll Book 1962
9042 *HOUSE FOR SALE* 1962 - dolls and furniture from #1248, no outfits for dolls.
9044 *PLAY CITY* stand-ups, 1963 catalog
9045 *TWO LITTLE GIRLS* 1964 - Big, Big Doll Book. Dolls new, clothes from #2610, #2915, and #2904. This book #9045 is pictured as it has reprints of its own.
9046 *PUNCH-OUT BAZAAR* - stand-ups and toys - 1965 catalog
9047 *BROTHER AND SISTER* 1965 catalog (9301) and (9302)
9047-P *BROTHER AND SISTER* 1967 (9302) and (9301)
9079 *INDOOR FUN ACTIVITY BOOK* 1968 - two pages of paper dolls to color
9101 *MIMI* - Clothes snap on (3905)
9102 *FAIRY PRINCESS* (1242)
9103 *THREE LIVIN DOLLS* (3903)
9104 *SUZY* 1962 - Box (5901)
9105 *PATTI* 1962 - Box (3921)
9106 *MOLLY* 1962 - Box (5908)
9107 *LIFE LIKE DOLLS* - Box - 1965 catalog (3903)
9108 *MAKE BELIEVE BEAUTY PARLOR* - Box - 1965 catalog. Large wipe-off face with four make-up crayons and make-up wigs. Not a paper doll.
9109 *KATHY* - 30" stand-up Doll 1962 (9986)
9110 *CECELIA* - 30" stand-up Doll 1962 (9985)
9111 *SALLY STORYBOOK* 1961 - Box (2610)
9118 *BETSY* - Box 1964 (date in Lowe records)
9119 *BABY DOLL* - Box 1964 (date in Lowe records) (2403)
9120 *DRESSMAKER SET* 1964 - Box (date in Lowe records) (2750 Elizabeth & 2751 Bonnie)
9121 *HELLO DOLLIES* - Box, 1965 catalog. Contained a Dress-a-doll Storybook of either #3944, #3945, #3946 or #3947 plus two small paper doll books which varied.
9211 *FUN BOX*, 1965 catalog - includes marionette and other punchouts
9212 *AROUND THE WORLD ACTIVITY BOOK* - Coloring and sticker fun, but does mention color slide punch-out. 1965 catalog
9301 *JACK* 1963
9302 *JILL* 1963
9302-P *JILL* 1963 (9302)
9302-P *JACK* 1963 (9301)
9310 *JACK* (9301)
9800 *JACK AND JILL* (9301 and 9302)
9985 *CECELIA MY KISSIN' COUSIN* 1960
9986 *KATHY* - 30" Doll 1962

The Merrill Publishing Company

The Merrill Publishing Company was formed in 1934 by Miss Marion Merrill and produced paper dolls, story books, coloring books and other books for children from the start. Recently found records show that Miss Merrill graduated from grammar school in 1916 and high school in Chicago in 1920. Later, she went on to graduate from Northwestern University with a Bachelor of Arts degree in 1933.

Miss Merrill had worked for the Western Printing and Lithographing Company (now Western Publishing Co.) through the latter years of the 1920's and up to 1933. Mrs. Samuel Lowe of the Lowe Publishing Company remembers that Marion had worked out of Western's Chicago office during the same time period (late Twenties, early Thirties) that she and her husband were also working for Western in Racine, Wisconsin. The Lowes left Western a few years after Miss Merrill had left. By 1933, Miss Merrill had rough-drafted some books that she had in mind and which she earnestly wanted to publish. She set out to find a reliable printer in Chicago who had the equipment and experience to produce top quality books. She was directed to the Regensteiner Corporation, developer of three and four color process printing.

In a book published in 1943 by Theodore Regensteiner*, an account is given of Miss Merrill's first visit to their office. During her interview, an agreement was worked out that Miss Merrill would submit six of her books in dummy form to a few head buyers for chain stores in New York, and, if she were able to get the buyers' approval, the Regensteiner Corporation would immediately proceed with the printing of a limited edition of each book. Needless to say Miss Merrill's books met with instant approval, and a 10-year contract was drawn up with the Regensteiner Corporation.

Those 10 years were very productive for Merrill, and an abundance of beautiful children's books were published. The Merrill Company's first books were *CAPTURING WILD ELEPHANTS*, #3480 and *BARNYARD BABIES IN THE ALPHABET*, #3481. Both are storybooks. The first paper doll book was *QUINTUPLETS, THE DIONNE BABIES*, #3488, 1935. The second paper doll book was *WEDDING OF THE PAPER DOLLS* #3497, 1935. In 1940 The Merrill Co. published two different sets of *GONE WITH THE WIND* #3404 and #3405 and in 1941 the *ZIEGFELD GIRL* #3466. All of these books are rare collectors items now. Through the years The Merrill Company produced over 160 paper doll books of which a small fraction are reprints.

When the contract agreement ended in December 1944, Miss Merrill had the company name changed from The Merrill Publishing Company to The Merrill Company Publishers. She found a new printer and went on to publish books for another twenty some years. Miss Marion Merrill died in 1978, and in April 1979, the company was sold to Jean Woodcock, a paper doll collector and author who now owns all of the company records and archives.

All Paper Dolls Pictured Are Copyrighted By The Merrill Publishing Company.

*Theodore Regensteiner. My First Seventy-five Years. Chicago, Regensteiner Corporation. 1943.

Merrill Publishing Company 1942 Spring and Summer catalog.

Courtesy of Jean Woodcock.

Courtesy of Jean Woodcock.

1542 *LITTLE BALLERINA* 1953. $5.00

Courtesy of Audrey Sepponen.

1543 *GOLDEN GIRL* 1953. $10.00

Courtesy of Audrey Sepponen.

1544 *JOHNNY, JANEY AND JUDY IN STORYBOOK LAND* 1952. $5.00

1546 *AROUND THE CLOCK WITH SUE AND DOT* 1952. $5.00

1547 *THE LITTLE FAIRY* 1951. $5.00

1548 *KITTY GOES TO KINDERGARTEN* 1956. $5.00

1548 *AMERICAN BEAUTY PAPER DOLLS* With Dresses Worn by White House Ladies 1951. $15.00

1549 *BIG 'N' LITTLE SISTER* 1951. $5.00

1549 *SALLY'S SILVER SKATES* 1956. $6.00

1550 *LET'S PLAY WITH THE BABY* 1948. $6.00

Courtesy of Virginia Crossley.

1551 *HIGH SCHOOL DOLLS* 1948. $10.00

1552 *PERT AND PRETTY* 1948. $10.00

1553 *THE HEAVENLY TWINS AND THEIR GUARDIAN ANGELS* 1948. $8.00

1554 *DOLLS FROM STORYLAND* 1948. $8.00

Courtesy of Virginia Crossley.

1555 *BRIDE AND GROOM* 1949. There are two editions of this book. One has eight pages of clothes and the other has six. Pictured is the eight page book. Both are #1555, and covers are identical, except the date is inside the eight page book and on the cover of the six page book. 8 page - $6.00; 6 page - $5.00

1556 *POLLY AND HER PLAYMATES* 1951. $5.00

1557 *THE JUDY PAPER DOLLS* 1951. $5.00

Courtesy of Audrey Sepponen.

1558 *BETTY GRABLE* 1951. There are two editions of the #1558 Betty Grable book. One has eight pages of outfits the other only six. Both have identical covers. The eight page book is pictured.. $35.00

1559 *THE PINK WEDDING* 1952. $8.00

Courtesy of Audrey Sepponen.

1560 *AIRLINER PILOT AND STEWARDESS* 1953. $7.00

Courtesy of Audrey Sepponen.

1560 *BETTY BLUE AND PATTY PINK* 1949. $8.00

#1560 Inside front cover of Betty Blue and Patty Pink.

Courtesy of Audrey Sepponen.

1561 *THE LITTLE FAMILY AND THEIR LITTLE HOUSE* 1949.
$12.00

#1561 Inside front cover of Little Family

1561 *B IS FOR BETSY* 1954 (and C is for Carol on back cover).
$5.00

1562 *CATHY GOES TO CAMP* 1954. $5.00

1562 *CHILDREN IN THE SHOE* 1949. $10.00   **Courtesy of Virginia Crossley**

#1562 Inside front cover of Children in the Shoe

1563 *ESTHER WILLIAMS* 1950. $35.00

Courtesy of Audrey Sepponen.

#1563 Inside front cover of Esther Williams

1563 *IN PETER PUMPKIN'S HOUSE* 1955. $5.00

Courtesy of Audrey Sepponen.

1564 *KAREN GOES TO COLLEGE* 1955. $5.00

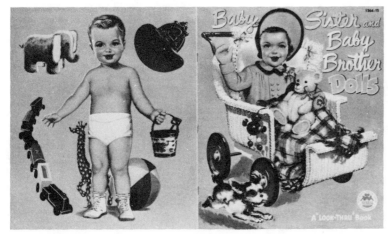

1564 *BABY SISTER AND BABY BROTHER DOLLS* 1950. $5.00

#1564 Inside front cover of Baby Sister - Baby Brother

Courtesy of Jean Woodcock

Courtesy of Audrey Sepponen.

2500 *CHILDREN OF OTHER LANDS* 1954. Activity Coloring Book. Contains many pages of paper dolls to be colored. $3.00

2553 *ESTHER WILLIAMS* 1953. Paper doll and coloring book. $35.00

2550 *ANN BLYTH* 1952. $35.00

Courtesy of Audrey Sepponen.

#2550 Inside front cover.

2551 *PIPER LAURIE* 1953. $35.00

Courtesy of Audrey Sepponen.

#2551 Inside front cover.

2552 *BETTY GRABLE* 1953. $35.00

Courtesy of Audrey Sepponen.
#2552 Inside front cover.

Courtesy of Virginia Crossley.

2562 *UMBRELLA GIRLS* 1956. $8.00

#2562 Inside front cover.

#2562 Inside back cover.

554 *JANET LEIGH* 1953. Paper doll and coloring book. $35.00

Courtesy of Audrey Sepponen.

2564 *LINDY-LOU 'N' CINDY-SUE* 1954. $8.00

#2564 Inside front and back covers.

2565 *CHILDREN 'ROUND THE WORLD* 1955. $8.00

#2565 Inside front cover.

#2565 Inside back cover.

Courtesy of Virginia Crossley.

2580 *HEAVENLY BLUE WEDDING* 1955. $7.00

#2580 Inside cardboard sheets of dolls.

2582 *6 AND SWEET 16* 1955. $6.00

#2582 Inside cardboard sheets of dolls.

2583 *PINK PROM TWINS* 1956. $5.00

Courtesy of Audrey Sepponen.

#2583 Inside cardboard sheets of dolls.

2584 *THE RANCH FAMILY* 1957. $5.00

#2584 Inside cardboard sheets of dolls.

3400 *COLLEGE STYLE* 1941. $15.00

Courtesy of Virginia Crossley.

2968 *LITTLE MISS CHRISTMAS AND HOLLY-BELLE* 1965.
$8.00

#2968 Inside front cover of folder type book.

#M3404   Courtesy of Betsy Slap.

#M3404

M3403 *STAND-UP DOLLS - HONEY AND BUNNY* 1936. $30.00

M3404 *NEW QUINTUPLETS DOLLS* 1936. $40.00 & up

3404 *GONE WITH THE WIND* 1940. $75.00 & up

Courtesy of Virginia Crossley.

Courtesy of Dot Trippel.

3405 *GONE WITH THE WIND* 1940. $75.00 & up

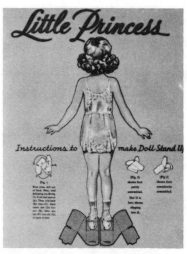

#3405 Reverse side of back cover.

3405 *THE LITTLE PRINCESS* 1936. $30.00.

3408 *GROWN-UP PAPER DOLLS* 1936. $20.00

3408 *SUB-DEB PAPER DOLLS* 1941. $20.00

Courtesy of Virginia Crossley.

3411 *BRIDE AND GROOM MILITARY WEDDING PARTY* 1941. $20.00

#3411 Inside front cover

3418 *SONJA HENIE* 1941. $50.00 & up

Courtesy of Audrey Sepponen.

3415 *DRUM MAJOR AND MAJORETTE* 1941. $18.00

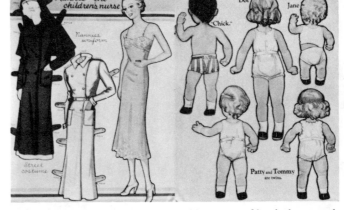

Courtesy of Audrey Sepponen.

3416 *DOLLS WE LOVE* 1936. $30.00

#3416 Reverse side of back cover and last page of book showing the nurse.

Courtesy of Audrey Sepponen.

3423 *AIRLINER PAPER DOLLS* 1941. $15.00

#3423 Inside front cover

Courtesy of Audrey Sepponen.

3425 *ARMY NURSE AND DOCTOR* 1942. $15.00

3424 *VICTORY VOLUNTEERS* 1942. $18.00

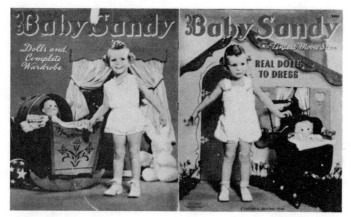

Courtesy of Emma Terry.

3428 *NAVY SCOUTS* 1942. $15.00

3426 *BABY SANDY* 1941. $40.00 & up

3426 *TWIN BABIES* 1942. $15.00

Courtesy of Pearl Silzly.

#3426 Inside front cover of Twin Babies

Courtesy of Pearl Silzly.

#3428 Inside front cover.

#3428 Inside back cover.

3428 *OUR NEW BABY* 1937. $18.00

Courtesy of Audrey Sepponen.

#3436 Back cover.

3436 *PAPER DOLL FAMILY AND THEIR TRAILER* 1938. $25.00

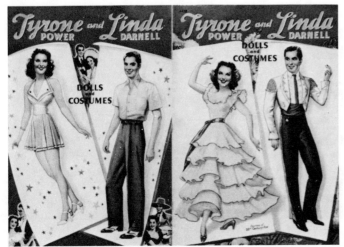

3440 *STAR BABIES* 1945. $12.00

3438 *TYRONE POWER AND LINDA DARNELL* 1941. $60.00 &
up

3441 *SEVEN AND SEVENTEEN* 1945. $12.00

3442 *BIG 'N' EASY* 1949. $7.00

Courtesy of Betsy Slap.

3442 *15 PUPPY-KITTY CUT-OUTS* 1938. $40.00

3443 *TEEN TOWN* 1946. $12.00

Courtesy of Audrey Sepponen.

3444 *PIG-TAILS* 1949. $6.00

3445 *THE COKE CROWD* 1946. $12.00

3444 *BABY SISTERS* 1938. $20.00

#3444 Baby Sisters - Inside front and back covers.

3444 *BLUE BONNET PAPER DOLLS* 1942. $20.00

#3444 Blue Bonnet - Inside front cover.

#3444 Blue Bonnet - Back inside flap.

3446 *THE SUSAN DOLL BOOK* 1950. $5.00

3446 *27 DANCING SCHOOL PAPER DOLLS* 1938. $30.00

3447 *BALLET DANCERS* 1947. $12.00

3448 *DREAM GIRL* 1947. $12.00

Courtesy of Audrey Sepponen.

Courtesy of Audrey Sepponen.

3449 *COWBOY AND COWGIRL* 1950. $5.00

3450 *THE TWO MARYS* 1950. $5.00

3455 *CRADLE TOTS* 1945. $12.00

3459 6 *GROWN-UP PAPER DOLLS* 1941. $12.00

Courtesy of Audrey Sepponen.

3459A *A PARTY OF 6 PAPER DOLLS* 1941. $12.00

3460 *JEANETTE MacDONALD* 1941. $60.00 & up

Courtesy of Audrey Sepponen.

3461 *JEANETTE MacDONALD COSTUME PARADE* 1942 (Paint book with paper doll). $25.00

3466 *HAPPY BIRTHDAY* 1939. $25.00

Courtesy of Emma Terry.

3466 *ZIEGFELD GIRL* 1941. $75.00 & up

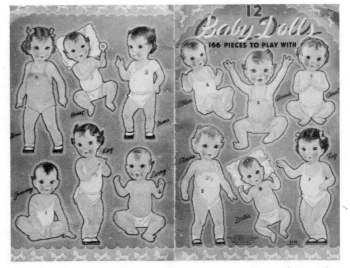

Courtesy of Betsy Slap.

3470 *12 BABY DOLLS* 1939. $25.00

3472 *MAKE CLOTHES FOR PATSY* 1941 (Make clothes for Bobby on back cover). $20.00

Courtesy of Emma Terry.

3475 *SONJA HENIE* 1939. $50.00 & up.

3472 *DOUBLE WEDDING* 1939. $25.00

Courtesy of Emma Terry. #3472 Inside back cover of Double Wedding.

#3472 Inside front cover of Double Wedding.

3477 *LIBERTY BELLES* 1943. $15.00

Courtesy of Virginia Crossley.

#3477 Inside front cover.

3477 *HIGH SCHOOL* 1940. $20.00

Courtesy of Audrey Sepponen.

3478 *RITA HAYWORTH* 1942. $60.00 & up.

Courtesy of Emma Terry.

3480 *DEANNA DURBIN* 1940. $50.00 & up

3481 *REAL BABY PAPER DOLLS* 1940. $20.00

Courtesy of Audrey Sepponen.

3482 *HEDY LAMARR* 1942. $60.00 & up.

Courtesy of Emma Terry.

3492 *SONJA HENIE* 1940. $75.00 & up.

3481 *SOLDIERS AND SAILORS HOUSE PARTY* 1943. $20.00

#3481 Inside front cover.

Courtesy of Emma Terry.
M3488 *QUINTUPLETS, THE DIONNE BABIES* 1935. $75.00 & up.

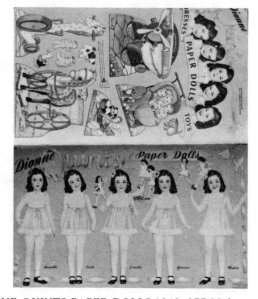

3488 *DIONNE QUINTS PAPER DOLLS* 1940. $75.00 & up.

Courtesy of Mary Kelley.
3492 *BOARDING SCHOOL* 1942. $15.00

Courtesy of Virginia Crossley.
M3497 *WEDDING OF THE PAPER DOLLS* 1935. $35.00

Courtesy of Shirley Hedge.

3500 *LET'S PLAY HOUSE WITH THE DIONNE QUINTS* 1940.
3500-A. Cecile $40.00

Courtesy of Shirley Hedge.

3500-B *ANNETTE.* $40.00

3500-C *EMILIE.* $40.00

Courtesy of Shirley Hedge.

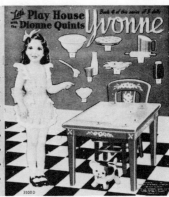

3500-D *YVONNE.* $40.00

Courtesy of Shirley Hedge.

3500-E *MARIE.* $40.00

Courtesy of Shirley Hedge.

4800 *ALICE FAY* 1941. $75.00 & up.

Courtesy of Emma Terry.

Courtesy of Emma Terry.

4804 *DEANNA DURBIN* 1941. $60.00 & up.

Courtesy of Audrey Sepponen.

4816 *BETTE DAVIS* 1942. $50.00 & up.

4827 *NEW BABY* 1943. $12.00

4828 *JILL AND HER TRUNK FULL OF CLOTHES* 1943. $12.00

4829 *TRUDY IN HER TEENS* 1943. $12.00

4851 *PAPER DOLL WEDDING* 1943 (dated 1944 on the inside). $15.00

4837 *210 THINGS TO DO* 1942. Activity book with two paper dolls. $5.00

Courtesy of Marilyn Johnson.

4853 *ANGEL BABY DOLLS* 1943. $15.00

Courtesy of Virginia Crossley.

4852 *GIRL PILOTS OF THE FERRY COMMAND* 1943. $15.00

4854 *SLUMBER PARTY* 1943. $15.00

Courtesy of Jean Woodcock.

4855 *NAVY GIRLS AND MARINES* 1943. $15.00

4856 *MAGAZINE COVER GIRLS* 1944 (America's Prettiest Girls). $15.00

4857 *WATCH ME GROW* 1944. $15.00

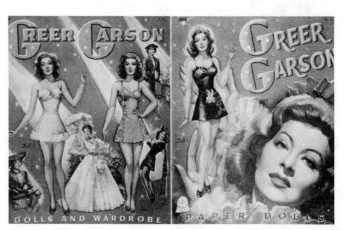

Courtesy of Audrey Sepponen.

4858 *GREER GARSON* 1944. $60.00 & up.

Courtesy of Virginia Crossley.

4859 *FIRST DATE* 1944. $15.00

4860 *BABY MINE* 1944. $15.00

4862 *SWEET 16* 1944. $15.00

Courtesy of Audrey Sepponen.

4865 *ROLLER RHYTHM* 1944. $15.00

4863 *BABY'S FIRST YEAR* 1945. $15.00

4866 *RIDE A PONY - JUDY AND JILL* 1944 (Jerry and Flash on the back cover). $15.00

List of Paper Dolls Published By The Merrill Publishing Company

This list contains all original and reprint books of paper dolls and related books published by the Merrill Company. If a book is a reprint it will have the number of the original book it is derived from in parenthesis following the title. If there should be more than one title for that number the book will be indicated unless it is obvious. All original paper doll books are pictured in the Merrill picture section.

1542 *LITTLE BALLERINA* 1953
1543 *GOLDEN GIRL* 1953
1544 *JOHNNY, JANEY AND JUDY IN STORYBOOK LAND* 1952
1545 *SIX LITTLE STEPPERS* 1953 (1562 - Children in the Shoe)
1546 *FOUR LITTLE GIRLS FROM SCHOOL* 1951/1957 (1556 - Polly)
1546 *AROUND THE CLOCK WITH SUE AND DOT* 1952
1547 *THE LITTLE FAIRY PAPER DOLLS* 1951
1547 *CINDERELLA, JACK AND JILL STORY FAVORITES* 1952/1957 (1544)
1548 *KITTY GOES TO KINDERGARTEN* 1956
1548 *AMERICAN BEAUTY PAPER DOLLS WITH DRESSES WORN BY WHITE HOUSE LADIES* 1951
1548 *FAIRY PRINCESS* 1951/1958 (1547 - Little Fairy)
1549 *SALLY'S SILVER SKATES* 1956
1549 *BIG 'N' LITTLE SISTER* 1951
1550 *LET'S PLAY WITH THE BABY* 1948
1550 *WHITE HOUSE PARTY DRESSES* 1961 (1548)
1551 *HIGH SCHOOL DOLLS* 1948
1551 *SKY BABIES* 1959 (3440)
1552 *PERT AND PRETTY* 1948
1552 *THREE ICE SKATING DOLLS* 1956/1960 (1549)
1553 *HEAVENLY TWINS AND THEIR GUARDIAN ANGELS* 1948
1553 *JANE, JEAN AND JOAN* 1950/1959 (3446 - Susan)
1554 *DOLLS FROM STORYLAND* 1948
1554 *BALLERINA DOLLS* 1953/1960 (1542)
1555 *BRIDE AND GROOM* 1949 - There are two editions of this book, one with eight pages of outfits and one with six. The covers and outfits are the same. The eight page book is dated on the inside first page and the six page book is dated on the front cover.
1556 *POLLY AND HER PLAYMATES* 1951
1556 *SCHOOL FRIENDS* 1956/1960 (1548 - Kitty)
1557 *THE JUDY PAPER DOLLS* 1951
1557 *AIRLINE HOSTESS AND PILOT* 1962 (1560)
1557 *GAY AND GAIL* 1953/1958 (1543)

1558 *PINK CLOUD BRIDE AND HER PINK WEDDING* 1952/-1961 (1559)
1558 *BETTY GRABLE* 1951 - There are two editions of this book, one with eight pages of outfits and one with six pages. The covers and outfits are the same.
1559 *PINK WEDDING* 1952.
1559 *JACKIE, JEFF AND JULIE* 1961 (1564 - Karen)
1560 *BETTY BLUE AND PATTY PINK* 1949
1560 *AIRLINER PILOT AND STEWARDESS* 1953
1560 *THIS IS SUZIE, HERE IS JO-ANN* 1962
1561 *THE LITTLE FAMILY AND THEIR LITTLE HOUSE* 1949
1561 *B IS FOR BETSY* 1954
1561 *JACK AND JILL* 1962 (1563 - Peter)
1562 *CHILDREN IN THE SHOE* 1949
1562 *CATHY GOES TO CAMP* 1954
1562 *DOLLS FROM STORYLAND* 1963 (1554)
1563 *ESTHER WILLIAMS* 1950
1563 *IN PETER PUMPKIN'S HOUSE* 1955
1564 *BABY SISTER AND BROTHER DOLLS* 1950
1564 *KAREN GOES TO COLLEGE* 1955
1565 *THIS IS LUCY LOCKET WHO LOST HER POCKET* 1949/1956 (3442 -Big and Easy)
1566 *MADGE 'N' MARGE 'N' LINDA 'N' LEE* 1951/1956 (1549 - Big and Little)
2500 *CHILDREN OF OTHER LANDS* 1954. Coloring book with paper dolls to color.
2550 *ANN BLYTH* 1952
2551 *PIPER LAURIE* 1953
2552 *BETTY GRABLE* 1953. Coloring book and paper dolls
2553 *ESTHER WILLIAMS* 1953. Coloring book and paper dolls
2554 *JANET LEIGH* 1953. Coloring book and paper dolls
2562 *UMBRELLA GIRLS* 1956
2564 *LINDY-LOU 'N' CINDY-SUE* 1954
2565 *CHILDREN 'ROUND THE WORLD* 1955
2570 *BETTY BLUE AND PATTY PINK* 1949/1958 (1560)

2571 *LET'S PLAY PAPER DOLLS* - Baby Sister and Baby Brother Dolls 1950/1958 (1564)
2571 *TWINS, BABY SISTER AND BABY BROTHER* 1950/1960 (1564)
2572 *SEVEN CHILDREN LIVE IN A SHOE* 1949/1958 (1562)
2580 *HEAVENLY BLUE WEDDING* 1955
2581 *CANDY AND HER COUSINS* 1961 (2564)
2582 *SIX AND SWEET SIXTEEN* 1955
2582 *BIG 'N' LITTLE SIX SISTERS* - Six and Sweet Sixteen 1955/1960 (2582-Above)
2583 *PINK PROM TWINS* 1956
2584 *THE RANCH FAMILY* 1957
2968 *LITTLE MISS CHRISTMAS AND HOLLY BELLE* 1965.
3400 *COLLEGE STYLE* 1941
3402 *MICKEY ROONEY PUNCHOUT* 1941 - Stand-ups
M3403 *STAND-UP DOLLS, HONEY AND BUNNY* 1936
M3404 *NEW QUINTUPLET DOLLS* 1936
3404 *GONE WITH THE WIND* 1940
3405 *THE LITTLE PRINCESS* 1936
3405 *GONE WITH THE WIND* 1940
3408 *SUB DEB* 1941
3408 *GROWN-UP PAPER DOLLS* 1936
3411 *BRIDE AND GROOM MILITARY WEDDING PARTY* 1941
3415 *DRUM MAJOR AND MAJORETTE* 1941
3415 *DRUM MAJOR AND MAJORETTE* 1942 - Has different front cover, otherwise same as the 1941 book.
3416 *DOLLS WE LOVE* 1936
3418 *SONJA HENIE* 1941
3423 *AIRLINER PAPER DOLLS* - Pilot and Stewardess 1941
3424 *VICTORY VOLUNTEERS* - Dolls and Uniforms 1942
3425 *ARMY NURSE AND DOCTOR* 1942
3426 *BABY SANDY* 1941
3426 *TWIN BABIES* 1942
3428 *OUR NEW BABY* 1937
3428 *NAVY SCOUTS* 1942
3430 *AMERICAN DEFENSE BATTLES* - stand-ups 1940
3436 *PAPER DOLL FAMILY AND THEIR TRAILER* 1938
3438 *TYRONE POWER AND LINDA DARNELL* 1941
3440 *STAR BABIES* 1945
3441 *SEVEN AND SEVENTEEN* - Big and Little Sister 1945
3442 *BIG 'N' EASY, DOLLS 'N' CLOTHES* 1949
3442 *15 PUPPY-KITTY CUT-OUTS* 1938
3443 *TEEN TOWN* 1946
3443 *BRIDE AND GROOM* 1949 (1555)
3444 *BABY SISTERS* 1938
3444 *BLUE BONNET PAPER DOLLS* 1942
3444 *PIG-TAILS* 1949
3445 *COKE CROWD* 1946
3445 *BONNIE AND BILLE* 1954 (1550 Let's Play with the Baby)
3446 *27 DANCING SCHOOL PAPER DOLLS* 1938
3446 *THE SUSAN DOLL BOOK* 1950
3447 *BALLET DANCERS* 1947
3447 *TRUDY IN HER TEENS* 1954 (1551 High School)
3448 *DREAM GIRL* 1947
3448 *DANCING DOLLS WITH FAMOUS COSTUMES* 1954 (3447 Ballet)
3449 *COWBOY AND COWGIRL* 1950
3450 *THE TWO MARYS* 1950
3451 *MY FIRST CUT-OUT BOOK* 1952 (1564 Baby Sister and Brother)
3452 *BECKY AND BETSY* 1952 (1560 Betty Blue)
3453 *SIX LITTLE STEPPERS* 1953 (1562 Children in the Shoe)
3454 *THE JONES FAMILY* 1953 (1561 Little Family)
3455 *CRADLE TOTS* 1945
3456 *GLAMOUR GIRLS, 9 DANCING DOLLS* 1953 (1552 Pert and Pretty)

3457 *ANGEL BABIES* 1953 (4853)
3458 *SHERRY AND ADELE, DIANE AND LYNNE* 1953 (3448 Dream Girl)
3459 *6 GROWN-UP PAPER DOLLS* 1941
3459 *COWGIRL JILL AND COWBOY JOE* 1950/1955 (3449)
3459A *A PARTY OF 6 PAPER DOLLS* 1941
3460 *JEANETTE MacDONALD* 1941
3460 *SALLY, SANDRA AND SUE* 1950/1955 (1557 Judy)
3461 *JEANETTE MacDONALD COSTUME PARADE PAINT BOOK* 1942 (with paper doll)
3461 *STORY BOOK DOLLS* 1948/1955 (1554)
3462 *BABYLAND* 1945/1950/1955 (3455)
3463 *JUDY AND JAN* - Dress-a-like 1950/1956 (3450)
3464 *PATTY'S PLAYTIME DOLLS* 1949/1956 (3444 Pig Tails)
3466 *HAPPY BIRTHDAY* 1939
3466 *ZIEGFELD GIRL* 1941
3470 *12 BABY DOLLS* 1939
3472 *DOUBLE WEDDING* 1939
3472 *MAKE CLOTHES FOR PATSY - MAKE CLOTHES FOR BOBBY* 1941
3475 *SONJA HENIE* 1939
3477 *HIGH SCHOOL* 1940
3477 *LIBERTY BELLES* 1943
3478 *RITA HAYWORTH - DANCING STAR* 1942
3480 *DEANNA DURBIN* 1940
3481 *REAL BABY PAPER DOLLS* 1940
3481 *SOLDIERS AND SAILORS HOUSE PARTY* 1943
3482 *GENE AUTRY* 1940 - Stand-ups
3482 *HEDY LAMARR* 1942
M3488 *QUINTUPLETS, THE DIONNE BABIES* 1935
3488 *DIONNE QUINTS PAPER DOLLS* 1940
3492 *SONJA HENIE* 1940
3492 *BOARDING SCHOOL* 1942
3495 *BIG FARM PUNCH-OUT BOOK* 1940 - stand-ups
M3497 *WEDDING OF THE PAPER DOLLS* 1935
3500A *LET'S PLAY HOUSE WITH THE DIONNE QUINTUPLETS* 1940 - Cecile
3500B *LET'S PLAY HOUSE WITH THE DIONNE QUINTUPLETS* 1940 - Annette
3500C *LET'S PLAY HOUSE WITH THE DIONNE QUINTUPLETS* 1940 - Emilie
3500D *LET'S PLAY HOUSE WITH THE DIONNE QUINTUPLETS* 1940 - Yvonne
3500E *LET'S PLAY HOUSE WITH THE DIONNE QUINTUPLETS* 1940 - Marie
4800 *ALICE FAY* 1941
4802 *GENE AUTRY PUNCH-OUT* 1941 - stand-ups
4804 *DEANNA DURBIN* 1941
4816 *BETTE DAVIS* 1942
4827 *NEW BABY* 1943
4828 *JILL AND HER TRUNK FULL OF CLOTHES* 1943
4829 *TRUDY IN HER TEENS* 1943
4837 *210 THINGS TO DO* 1942 (has two paper dolls)
4851 *PAPER DOLL WEDDING* 1943 date on cover, 1944 date on inside page.
4852 *GIRL PILOTS OF THE FERRY COMMAND* 1943
4853 *ANGEL BABY DOLLS* 1943
4854 *SLUMBER PARTY* 1943
4855 *NAVY GIRLS AND MARINES* 1943
4856 *MAGAZINE COVER GIRLS - AMERICA'S PRETTIEST GIRLS* 1944
4857 *WATCH ME GROW, FROM ONE TO SIX YEARS OLD* 1944
4858 *GREER GARSON* 1944
4859 *FIRST DATE* 1944
4860 *BABY MINE* 1944
4862 *SWEET 16* 1944
4863 *BABY'S FIRST YEAR* 1945
4865 *ROLLER RHYTHM, HIGH SCHOOL DOLLS ON SKATES* 1944
4866 *RIDE A PONY JUDY AND JILL, RIDE A PONY JERRY AND FLASH* 1944

Merrill Publishing Company Coloring Books with Paper Dolls

The following is a list of coloring books, published by the Merrill Company, that included some pages of paper dolls to be colored. Some of the books contain the same paper dolls while others may have the same paper dolls with additional paper dolls that are different.

Two of the books #4837 *210 THINGS TO DO* and #2500 *CHILDREN OF OTHER LANDS* are pictured in the Merrill picture section.

My thanks to Jean Woodcock for this coloring book list.

1574 *RAINY DAY FUN* 1951
1574 *FUN ON A RAINY DAY* 1956
2500 *CHILDREN OF OTHER LANDS* 1954
2500 *BOYS AND GIRLS FROM FAR AWAY LANDS* 1956
2500 *CHILDREN ROUND THE WORLD* 1959
2502 *MY FIRST BOOK OF BIBLE STORIES* 1953
2502 *FIRST BIBLE STORIES* 1954
2503 *THE HAPPY BOOK* 1952
2503 *JOLLY FUN BOOK* 1954
2505 *THE CHAMP* 1954
2510 *GIANT SIZE BUSY BOOK* 1951

2510 *SUNNY HOURS ON A RAINY DAY* 1955
2511 *SMILES* 1952
2516 *HAPPY HOURS ON A RAINY DAY* 1954
2526 *EASY COLORING* 1955
M3401 *READ, COLOR, CUT AND PASTE* 1936
3431 *PLAYTIME READING* 1937
3454 *READ AND COLOR* 1939
3478 *RAINY DAY FUN* 1940
4837 *210 THINGS TO DO* 1942
4942 *GREAT BIG PLAYTIME BUSY BOOK* 1958
4942 *GREAT BIG PLAYTIME BUSY BOOK* 1962

Photo Index